PERGAMON INTERNATIONAL LIBRARY
of Science, Technology, Engineering and Social Studies
The 1000-volume original paperback library in aid of education,
industrial training and the enjoyment of leisure
Publisher: Robert Maxwell, M.C.

THE POLITICS OF AFRICAN AND MIDDLE EASTERN STATES
An Annotated Bibliography

THE PERGAMON TEXTBOOK
INSPECTION COPY SERVICE

An inspection copy of any book published in the Pergamon International
Library will gladly be sent to academic staff without obligation for their
consideration for course adoption or recommendation. Copies may be retained
for a period of 60 days from receipt and returned if not suitable. When a
particular title is adopted or recommended for adoption for class use and the
recommendation results in a sale of 12 or more copies, the inspection copy may
be retained with our compliments. If after examination the lecturer decides that
the book is not suitable for adoption but would like to retain it for his personal
library, then a discount of 10% is allowed on the invoiced price. The Publishers
will be pleased to receive suggestions for revised editions and new titles to be
published in this important International Library.

Other Titles of Interest

BURLEY, J. & TREGEAR, P.	African Development and Europe
HALLETT, R.	People and Progress in West Africa
OSBORNE, M.	Region of Revolt: Focus on Southeast Asia
CLARKE, J.I.	Population Geography and the Developing Countries
O'CONNOR, A.M.	The Geography of Tropical African Development
BROKENSHA, D. & CROWDER, M.	Africa in the Wider World
WEST, J.	Alternatives in Development: Is Europe Responding to Third World Needs?
LEON., D.	The Kibbutz: A New Way of Life
SCHWARTZ, P.N.	Confrontation or Cooperation?
WILLIAMS, D.	To Be Or Not To Be: A Question of Survival
SCHAFF, A.	History and Truth
PITT, D.	The Social Dynamics of Development
SLATER, D.	Underdevelopment and Spatial Inequality: Approaches to the Problems of Regional Planning in the Third World
BROWN, L.R. & ECKHOLM, E.P.	By Bread Alone
BROWN, L.R.	In the Human Interest: A Strategy to Stabilize World Population
MAXWELL, N.	China's Road to Development
MOHTADI, M.F.	Man and His Environment, Vol.2
RABINOWITCH, V. & RABINOWITCH, E.	Views on Science, Technology and Development
SALAS, R.	People: An International Choice. The Multilateral Approach to Population

---

WORLD DEVELOPMENT

Chairman of the Editorial Board: PAUL P. STREETEN, Oxford

It is the purpose of this journal to expose and analyse those forces which both impede and promote development in its widest sense.

Published monthly
1977 Annual subscription $100, including postage and insurance

THE POLITICS OF AFRICAN
AND
MIDDLE EASTERN STATES

An Annotated Bibliography

COMPILED BY

ANNE GORDON DRABEK
AND
WILFRID KNAPP

PERGAMON PRESS
OXFORD · NEW YORK · TORONTO · SYDNEY
PARIS · FRANKFURT

024566

U.K.	Pergamon Press Ltd., Headington Hill Hall, Oxford, OX3 0BW, England
U.S.A.	Pergamon Press Inc., Maxwell House, Fairview Park, Elmsford, New York 10523, U.S.A.
CANADA	Pergamon of Canada Ltd., 75 The East Mall, Toronto, Ontario, Canada
AUSTRALIA	Pergamon Press (Aust.) Pty. Ltd., 19a Boundary Street, Rushcutters Bay, N.S.W. 2011, Australia
FRANCE	Pergamon Press SARL, 24 rue des Ecoles, 75240 Paris, Cedex 05, France
WEST GERMANY	Pergamon Press GmbH, 6242 Kronberg-Taunus, Pferdstrasse 1, Frankfurt-am-Main, West Germany

Copyright © 1976 Institute of Commonwealth Studies

All Rights Reserved. No part of this publication may be reproduced, stored in a retrieval system, or transmitted in any form or by any means: electronic, electrostatic, magnetic tape, mechanical, photocopying, recording or otherwise, without permission in writing from the publishers

First edition 1976

Library of Congress Cataloging in Publication Data

Gordon Drabek, Anne

The politics of African and Middle Eastern states.

(Pergamon international library of science, technology, engineering and social studies)
Bibliography: p
1. Africa—Politics and government—Bibliography.
2. Near East—Politics and government—Bibliography
1. Knapp, Wilfrid, joint author. II. Title.
Z3508.P6D7 1976 [JQ1879.A15] 016.3209'6 76-26649
ISBN 0-08-020583-6 (pbk.)
ISBN 0-08-020584-4

In order to make this volume available as economically and rapidly as possible the author's typescript has been reproduced in its original form. This method unfortunately has its typographical limitations but it is hoped that they in no way distract the reader.

Z
3508
.P6D7
1976

Printed in Great Britain by A. Wheaton & Co., Exeter

CONTENTS

INTRODUCTION

This annotated bibliography covers the geographical regions of Africa and the Middle East. It is hoped that this will be the first of a series, eventually to include all regions of the developing world. This volume is organized in such a way to facilitate the comparative study of political development.

We have concerned ourselves largely with the evolution of states after independence. However, we have included a number of historical studies which treat the colonial period and advent to independence in order to provide some background to the continuing influence of former colonial powers over the political development of their former colonies.

The majority of the sources treat all aspects of internal political development: economic and social factors, political factors, governmental structures, colonial heritage, political parties, interest groups (tribal, religious, social, etc.), and ideologies (nationalism, Pan-Africanism, communism, social-ism, etc.). In listing sources providing biographies and per-sonal statements of political leaders, we hope to assist an understanding of the nature of political leadership in these countries and of the role played by these individuals in poli-tical development. Finally, we have dealt with sources on international politics whose concern is primarily African and Middle Eastern states, including such issues as boundary con-flicts, regional integration, international organization and relations with the developed world.

We would like to thank Mr. Bob Townsend, librarian of the Institute of Commonwealth Studies, Oxford, for his consid-erable and patient assistance, and Mr. Tony Kirk-Greene and Professor Leonard Thompson for their help in providing sources on their particular regions of interest.

Anne Gordon Drabek
Wilfrid Knapp

June 1976

SELECT BIBLIOGRAPHY OF WORKS
ON POLITICAL DEVELOPMENT

ALMOND, Gabriel A., and James S. COLEMAN, eds.
The Politics of Developing Areas (Princeton, N.J.:
Princeton University Press, 1970)

ALMOND, Gabriel A., and G. Bingham POWELL, Jr.
Comparative Politics: a developmental approach (Boston
and Toronto: Little, Brown, 1966)

APTER, David E.
The Politics of Modernization (Chicago and London:
University of Chicago Press, 1967)

DEAN, Vera Micheles
The Nature of the Non-Western World (New York: Mentor
Books, New American Library of World Literature, Inc.,
1957)

DODD, C.H.
Political Development (London: Macmillan, 1972)

FINER, S.E.
Comparative Government (London: Allen Lane, The Penguin
Press, 1970)

FINKLE, Jason L., and Richard W. GABLE, eds.
Political Development and Social Change (New York:
Wiley, 1966)

HUNTINGTON, Samuel P.
Political Order in Changing Societies (New Haven and
London: Yale University Press, 1968)

KAUTSKY, John H.
Communism and the Politics of Development (New York:
Wiley, 1968)

KAUTSKY, John H., ed.
Political Change in Underdeveloped Countries: nationalism
and communism (New York: Wiley, 1966)

LERNER, Daniel
The Passing of Traditional Society: modernizing the
Middle East (New York: The Free Press of Glencoe;
London: Collier-Macmillan, 1964)

MEHDEN, Fred R. von der
Politics of Developing Nations (Englewood Cliffs, N.J.:
Prentice-Hall, 1964)

MOORE, Barrington, Jr.
    Social Origins of Dictatorship and Democracy: lord and
    peasant in the making of the modern world   (London:
    Allen Lane, The Penguin Press, 1967)

PYE, Lucian W.
    Aspects of Political Development   (Boston: Little, Brown,
    1966)

RUSTOW, Dankwart A.
    A World of Nations: problems of modernization   (Washing-
    ton, D.C.: Brookings Institution, 1967)

SHILS, Edward
    Political Development in New States   (The Hague: Mouton,
    1965)

WORSLEY, Peter
    The Third World: a vital new force in international
    affairs   (London: Weidenfeld & Nicolson, 1964)

AFRICA-GENERAL

A. POLITICAL HISTORY

DUIGNAN, Peter, and L.H. GANN, eds.
  Colonialism in Africa 1870-1960: Volume 2, The History
  and Politics of Colonialism 1914-60 (Cambridge: Cambridge University Press, 1970)   563 pp.

  Attempts to 'strike a balance between Eurocentric and
  Afrocentric approach'; takes topical approach rather
  than chronological. Deals with subjects such as emerging black elites, policies of European powers, impact of
  white settlement on certain areas, military in Africa,
  and decolonization.

DUIGNAN, Peter, and L.H. GANN, eds.
  Colonialism in Africa 1870-1960: Volume 5, A Bibliogra-
  phical Guide to Colonialism in Sub-Saharan Africa
  (Cambridge: Cambridge University Press, 1973)   552 pp.

  Excellent annotated bibliography. Sources divided by
  colonial power and by individual country.

EMERSON, Rupert
  From Empire to Nation: the rise to self-assertion of
  Asian and African peoples (Cambridge, Mass.: Harvard
  University Press, 1960)   466 pp.

  Argues that impact of World War II made self-determination a principle for those peoples living under colonial
  empires and caused decline of colonial imperialism.
  Defines concept of 'nation' and then discusses relationship between nationalism and democracy in context of
  evolution of new states.

HODGKIN, Thomas
  Nationalism in Colonial Africa (London: Frederick
  Muller, Ltd., 1956)   216 pp.
  Bibliography.

  Classic analysis of origins of modern political parties
  and activity in Africa. Considers effects of different
  colonial policies practiced by European powers, then
  examines institutions through which nationalism operates
  and ideas by which it is influenced.

HUNTER, Guy
<u>The New Societies of Tropical Africa: a selective study</u>
(London: Oxford University Press, 1962)   376 pp.
Bibliography.

Characterizes interactions between Europeans and African elites during colonial period and towards independence, especially in context of economic relations;
traces evolution of African economies and roles of various African participants, i.e., as villagers, traders,
industrial workers, managers, as well as role of total
educational process in formation of labour force and
growth of 'new societies'.

KIRKWOOD, Kenneth
<u>Britain and Africa</u>   (London: Chatto & Windus, 1965)
235 pp.

First three chapters present chronological view of developments from entry of Britain into Africa until 1964
(emphasizing 1914-64).   Then examines relations between
Britain and three separate regions of Africa: Southern,
West, Eastern.   Finally, assesses potential for future
constructive relationship and partnership.

MACKENZIE, W.J.M., and Kenneth ROBINSON, eds.
<u>Five Elections in Africa: a group of electoral studies</u>
(Oxford: Clarendon Press, 1960)   496 pp.

Provides election studies in context of transition of
power and political development in African colonies:
compares French and British methods, large vs small
units, absence of settlers vs presence of settlers of
different types, etc.   Case studies are: Western Region,
Nigeria (1956); Eastern Region, Nigeria (1957); Sierra
Leone (1957); Senegal (1957); Kenya (1957).

TURNER, V.
<u>Colonialism in Africa 1870-1960: Volume 3, Profiles of
Change</u>   (Stanford, Calif.: Stanford University Press,
1971)   455 pp.
Bibliography (for each chapter).

Studies effects of colonial rule on various aspects of
African society -- emphasis is not on political effects
and responses.

B. POLITICAL SYSTEMS, GOVERNMENT

ADU, Amishadai L.
  The Civil Service in Commonwealth Africa   (London:
  George Allen & Unwin, 1969)   253 pp.

  Written by member of Ghanaian civil service. Argues
  that no fundamental changes in structure of civil service were possible while civil services were trying to
  take on additional tasks after independence; also, accelerated nationalization of personnel was more effect-
  ively accomplished if they were introduced into well-
  established and recognized structures; as period of
  transition nears end, thought is being given to policies for reform in government machinery.

ADU, Amishadai L.
  The Civil Service in New African States   (London:
  George Allen & Unwin, 1965)   242 pp.

  Predecessor of above book. Studies problems of trans-
  forming civil services from colonial pattern to nation-
  ally-oriented service, and from being controlled mainly
  by expatriate senior staff to an indigenously based one.
  Concerned with experiences of former British colonies
  in East and West Africa.

ALDERFER, Harold F.
  Local Government in Developing Countries   (New York:
  McGraw-Hill Book Co., 1964)   251 pp.

  Outlines form and structure of different countries'
  local government, relation between local and national
  governments, local elections, local government finance,
  urban government, and other specific problems. Dis-
  tinguishes especially between French pattern, English
  pattern, Soviet model, and traditional residues.

CARTER, Gwendolen, ed.
  African One-Party States   (Ithaca, New York: Cornell
  University Press, 1962)   501 pp.
  Bibliography.

  Complements her book, Five African States. Compares six
  countries (Tunisia, Senegal, Guinea, Ivory Coast,
  Liberia, Tanganyika) which have had similar structural
  responses to needs of independence and unity but because of varying factors their one-party systems are
  based on different ideologies and strategies. Weakness
  of book is that it was written soon after independence,

and states had little time to evolve coherent political systems.

CARTER, Gwendolen, ed.
    Five African States: responses to diversity (Ithaca, New York: Cornell University Press, 1963; London: Pall Mall Press, 1964)   643 pp.
    Bibliography.

    Five states are Congo, Dahomey, Cameroon Federal Republic, Rhodesias and Nyasaland, South Africa. Contains socio-political survey of each country including historical background of colonial period. Each study is organized in same way and is therefore useful for comparative purposes, especially emphasizing response to diversity in society.

CARTER, Gwendolen, ed.
    National Unity and Regionalism in Eight African States (Ithaca, New York: Cornell University Press, 1966) 565 pp.
    Bibliography.

    Countries are Nigeria, Niger, Uganda, Ethiopia, Congo, Gabon, Central African Republic, Chad. Studies based on idea that current importance of intranational or supranational regionalisms is conditioned by degree of cohesion possessed by national administrations and/or political party structures; author considers historical political and economic factors underlying conflict. Essays cover some states on which there is paucity of material in English.

CURRIE, David P., ed.
    Federalism and the New Nations of Africa (Chicago: University of Chicago Press, 1964)   440 pp.

    Series of papers from symposium at University of California Law School Center for Legal Research; each paper followed by discussion. First section puts problems of federalism into historical perspective in Africa; following sections discuss economic, legal and international aspects of federalism, based on experience of countries outside Africa i.e. US, Canada, Europe.

DAVIDSON, Basil
    Which Way Africa? The Search for a New Society (Penguin African Library; Harmondsworth, Middlesex: Penguin Books, Ltd., 1971) Third edition. 270 pp.
    Bibliography.

Explains and discusses some leading African ideas on
political and economic development. Assesses progress
made by newly independent countries in achieving some
degree of stability and political development and analyzes hindrances faced. Chapter on neo-imperialism
discusses threat of white-supremacy rule in southern
Africa. Cites as challenge of 1970s problem of 'unification' at intra- and inter-territorial levels. Appendix
provides text of OAU charter.

DESCHAMPS, Herbert J.
Les institutions politiques de l'Afrique Noire (Paris:
Presses Universitaires de France, 1970) Third edition.
128 pp.

Considers political institutions in three stages: traditional, colonial and new independent states.

DORO, M.E., and N.M. STULTZ, eds.
Governing in Black Africa: perspectives on new states
(Englewood Cliffs, N.J.: Prentice Hall, 1970)   362 pp.
Bibliography.

Uses systems approach to political analysis in attempt-
ing to illustrate political processes that are typical
in contemporary Africa, but stresses individuality of
each state. Includes sections on determinants of political behaviour, agencies of modernization and mobilization, structure and processes of government, national
integration, international affairs.

DUMONT, Rene
False Start in Africa (London: Andre Deutsch, 1966)
320 pp.

Published first in French under title L'Afrique Noire
Est Mal Partie (1962). Discusses why tropical Africa,
after a tentative pre-colonial start, seems to be
marking time. Argues that although European colonialists are largely to blame, Africans have 'taken over'
now; discusses obstacles hindering current efforts at
industrial and agricultural development (both tradi-
tion-rooted ones and modern ones). As agronomist,
emphasizes problems in agricultural sector. Also
advocates common front in Africa, especially regarding
economic relations with developed countries. Conclusions are relatively optimistic, though conditional.

KUPER, L., and M.G. SMITH, eds.
  Pluralism in Africa (Berkeley: University of California
  Press, 1969)   546 pp.
  Bibliography (28 pp.).

  Papers attempt to arrive at a theoretical framework and
  definitions for further study of so-called plural societies, relating it to question of integrating such
  societies into a national political unit; also includes
  several case studies.

LOFCHIE, Michael F., ed.
  The State of the Nations: constraints on development in
  independent Africa (Berkeley: University of California
  Press, 1971)   305 pp.
  Bibliography.

  Approach is primarily political, emphasizing parameters
  of political choice as limited by a variety of external,
  domestic and historical constraints and, in particular,
  future political development as hindered by inadequate
  institutional capacity. Uses various country case
  studies.

MARKOVITZ, Irving Leonard
  African Politics and Society (New York: The Free Press,
  1970)   485 pp.
  Bibliography.

  Considers dynamics of societies making transition from
  colonial dependency to independence, and from traditional tribal units to modern nation-states; articles are
  problem-oriented. Divides political development of
  Africa into three stages: struggle for independence,
  consolidation of power, reorganization of society.
  Provides translations from six French articles previously unavailable in English.

MORGAN, E. Philip, ed.
  The Administration of Change in Africa: essays in the
  theory and practice of development administration in
  Africa (New York: Dunellen Publishing Co., 1974)
  420 pp.

  Most of papers were prepared for symposium at Syracuse
  University in May 1970. Divided into sections on theoretical perspectives on development and administration
  in general, on the African context of change, on case
  studies of development administration in Africa, and on
  relation between theory and practice.

NWABUEZE, B.O.
   Constitutionalism in the Emergent States   (London: C.
   Hurst and Co., 1973)   316 pp.

   Author is Nigerian academic lawyer. Studies nature of
   constitutions in new states, emphasizing such concepts
   as supremacy and legitimacy; uses Nigeria as case
   study as well as several other countries. In discussing
   relationship between national unity and constitutionalism, presents instances of constitutional breakdown
   such as emergencies, coups d'etat and secession.

NWABUEZE, B.O.
   Presidentialism in Commonwealth Africa   (London: C.
   Hurst and Co., 1974)   442 pp.
   Bibliography.

   Book tries to make thorough analysis of formal structure
   of presidential rule: nature of executive power, African
   adaptations of parliamentary to presidential government,
   centralism in government organization and president's
   role. Also discusses one-party state, subordination of
   legislature, relationship between centralism/president-
   ialism and human rights of individuals. Compares and
   assesses presidential constitutions in terms of their
   appropriateness for encouraging development.

POTHOLM, Christian P.
   Four African Political Systems   (Englewood Cliffs, N.J.:
   Prentice-Hall, 1970)   296 pp.

   Book designed for courses on comparative politics and
   political development: presents in comparative framework
   four political systems -- Tanzania, South Africa, Ivory
   Coast, Somalia. Systems compared in terms of decision-
   making, systemic capabilities and goal formation.
   Countries chosen as examples of political typologies
   with relevance outside their own boundaries.

RIVKIN, Arnold
   Nation-Building in Africa: problems and prospects
   (New Brunswick, N.J.: Rutgers University Press, 1969)
   312 pp.
   Bibliography.

   Discusses problems of nation-building in terms of geo-
   political situation, state structure(one-party state,
   role of military, role of modernizing oligarchical
   state, role of federalism), political systems (role of

rule of law, role of independent institutions), etc.
Considers prospects in terms of special case studies.
Finally, compares prospects in Africa with other devel-
oping areas.

RIVKIN, Arnold, ed.
Nations by Design: institution building in Africa
(Garden City, N.Y.: Anchor Books, Doubleday & Co., Inc.,
1968)   386 pp.

Author's introduction emphasizes critical importance of
institutional framework in establishing essential pre-
conditions of development: state-building, nation-building, economy-building, technological revolution, and
social restructuring. Also concerned with institutional
balance. Uses historical perspective regarding Sudan
and Senegal as case studies of development institutions,
especially integration of traditional and modern elements of structures.

SMITH, T.E.
Elections in Developing Countries   (London: Macmillan,
1960)   278 pp.
Bibliography.

Study of electoral codes which had been introduced by
British in colonies of Africa prior to independence;
attempts to evaluate how these electoral systems have
worked in practice. Does not, however, discuss broader
questions of role of democratic government in Africa or
logic of transferring British institutions onto African
societies.

SPIRO, Herbert J.
Africa: the primacy of politics   (New York: Random
House, 1966)   212 pp.

Articles deal with question: are political considerations accorded greater importance than economic, social,
cultural and other nonpolitical considerations, both
inside Africa and in Africa's relations with rest of
the world? Includes case studies of Congo and Southern
Nigeria, discussion of mass party regimes and of African
politics at the United Nations.

SPIRO, Herbert J., ed.
Patterns of African Development: five comparisons
(Englewood Cliffs, N.J.: Prentice-Hall, 1967)   144 pp.

Considers theoretical bases of comparative politics

(especially application of analogies), special features
of African nationalism, comparative modernization in
Japan and Africa, distinctions between borrowed political theory and original political practice in Africa,
and an explanation of political development as the development of African politics. Essays by Friedrich, Abu-
Lughod, Welch, Mazrui, Spiro.

SYMONDS, John Richard Charters
    The British and Their Successors: a study in the devel-
    opment of government services in the new states (London:
    Faber & Faber, 1966)   287 pp.
    Bibliography.

    Regional comparative study: India and Ceylon, West Afri-
    ca, East Africa. Traces interaction of different influ-
    ences and attitudes on development of government ser-
    vices in dependent territories, e.g. education and
    localization policy.

THIAM, Doudou
    Le Federalisme Africain: ses principes et ses regles
    (Paris: Presence Africaine, 1972)   101 pp.

    Author is former foreign minister of Senegal. Book
    stems from course given at Academie de Droit Interna-
    tional de la Haye in 1969. Describes evolution from
    territorial federalism to state federalism, including
    cultural, economic and political factors; outlines means
    of classification of different African organizations
    and their institutions.

WALLERSTEIN, Immanuel
    Africa: the politics of independence (New York: Vintage
    Books, Random House, 1961)   179 pp.
    Bibliography.

    Concerned with two central questions in the 'interpre-
    tive essay': (1) ways in which social structures gener-
    ate social conflict within themselves and under what
    conditions this conflict results in revolution which
    overthrows the structure; (2) ways in which social stru-
    ctures hold themselves together, acquire loyalty of
    subjects in complex economy where interests of citizens
    vary widely.

WRIGGINS, W. Howard
    The Ruler's Imperative: strategies for political survi-
    val in Asia and Africa (New York: Columbia University
    Press, 1969)   275 pp.

Focuses on political strategies used by leaders in the
'aggregation of power' and in building their supporting
coalition -- a rather uncommon approach in literature on
political development; discusses eight separate strategies and provides example of each.

YOUNGER, Kenneth
The Public Service in New States   (London: Oxford University Press, 1960)   113 pp.

Describes transition from 1954 onward in adapting colonial service (British) to new situation in which dependencies approached self-government/independence, and
burden of administration transferred to locally recruit-
ed officials.   Includes case studies of Nigeria, Camer-
oons, Ghana, Malaya, Sudan.   Annexes give statistics
regarding composition of administrative staff.

C. POLITICAL PARTIES, INTEREST GROUPS AND IDEOLOGIES

AINSLIE, Rosalynde
The Press in Africa: communications past and present
(London: Victor Gollancz Ltd., 1966)   256 pp.

Examines evolution of media in Africa; treats problem of
creating national newspapers independent of foreign
agencies (correspondents, etc.) for its collection of
news; discusses role of government vis-a-vis press and
press freedom in general, and question of press audience
and creation of truly mass media(not just for elite).

ARNAULT, Jacques
Du Colonialisme au Socialisme (Paris: Editions Sociales,
1966)   309 pp.

Author has chosen six countries (North Vietnam, Cuba,
Algeria, Guinea, Ghana and Mali) as examples of former
colonies which have chosen socialism of different types
rather than continue with colonial capitalist system;
compares socialist systems as they have evolved in
those countries and analyzes their potential and meaning.

BADIAN, Seydou
Les Dirigeants d'Afrique Noire Face a Leur Peuple
(Paris: Francois Maspero, 1964)   185 pp.

Author is former Mali minister for development. Discusses, from point of view of militant socialist, post-
independence problem of some African countries in ach-
eiving situation where power is really in hands of
Africans. Speaks of role of African leaders as

mobilizers of population, and sees legitimacy of single
party in traditional social structure.

BEBLER, Anton
Military Rule in Africa: Dahomey, Sierra Leone, Ghana,
Mali (New York: Praeger, 1973) 259 pp.

Author describes military takeovers in each of four West
African countries: analyzes relationship between socio-
political environment and military, impact of junta's
rule upon civilian policy, and dynamics of civilian-
military coalitions.

BELING, Willard A., ed.
The Role of Labor in African Nation-Building (Proceed-
ings of the Institue of World Affairs, Volume XLI; New
York: Praeger, 1968) 204 pp.

Examines role of labour after independencq: conference
papers discuss political status of unions, role of labour in new 'socialist' states, economic role of labour
in nation-building, labour's role in 'supranation-build-
ing' and in international affairs. Papers tend to be
constructively critical.

BELL, Wendell and Walter E. FREEMAN, eds.
Ethnicity and Nation-Building: comparative, internation-
al and historical perspectives (Beverly Hills/London:
Sage Publications, 1974) 400 pp.

Papers stem largely from International Studies Association conference, San Juan, Puerto Rico, March 1970.
Book is concerned with defining theoretical concept of
ethnicity, analyzing what other cleavages and conflicts
are associated with ethnicity, and studying problems of
nation-building, of equality and inequality and of self-
determination. See particularly Lemarchand, Butler,
McKown on African states.

BIENEN, Henry, ed.
The Military and Modernization (Chicago: Aldine-Ather-
ton, 1971) 242 pp.
Bibliography.

Relates in general to developing countries. Studies
potential of military as ruling force and as modernizing
force in society; in particular, studies societal origin
of members of military and its implications for policy.

BIENEN, Henry, ed.
The Military Intervenes: case studies in political development (New York: Russell Sage Foundation, 1968) 175 pp.

Problematic issue central to this book covers conditions under which military intervenes, mechanisms of intervention, and consequences. Editor concludes on basis of case study evidence that there exist powerful constraints which narrow role of military per se as effective agents of political change. However, case studies (Ethiopia, East Africa, Korea, Turkey, Argentina) are not comprehensive.

CAUTE, David
Fanon (London: Fontana, 1970)   106 pp.
Bibliography.

Sympathetic analysis of ideas of Frantz Fanon -- characterized as an 'intransigent revolutionary idealist'.

COLEMAN, G.J.S. and C.G. ROSBERG, eds.
Political Parties and National Integration in Tropical Africa (Berkeley/Los Angeles: University of California Press, 1966)   730 pp.
Bibliography.

Through study of political parties and other politically relevant aggregates and associations in various African countries, attempts to draw some conclusions about role of political parties and other groups in functioning and development of new African societies and political systems.

Commission Internationale d'Histoire des Mouvements Sociaux et des Structures Sociales
Mouvements Nationaux d'Independence et Classes Populaires aux XIXe et XXe Siecles en Occident et en Orient (Paris: Librairie Armand Colin, 1971)   720 pp.
Bibliography. Two volumes.

Volume II is most relevant to African nationalist movements (other sections provide interesting comparisons); treat such issues as rural peasant participation in nationalist movements and larger questions of mass political participation and mobilization. Authors are well-known scholars in the field.

DAVIES, Ioan
African Trade Unions (Penguin African Library; Penguin

Books, 1966)   256 pp.

Author tries to establish patterns of union role in
African societies; argues that although industrial labour is still a minority group, they hold strategic
place in developing economies. Studies union bargaining
power -- both those in opposition to ruling government
and those in context of one-party states. Makes general
survey of achievements and failures of trade unions in
Africa.

EMMERSON, Donald K., ed.
    Students and Politics in Developing Nations   (London:
    Pall Mall Press, 1968)   444 pp.

Comparative study of political attitudes and behaviour
of university students; includes, for Africa, case
studies of Algeria, Congo, Ghana and South Africa, plus
examples from Asia and Latin America. Attempts to place
student politics in context of national political scene
and tries to assess its impact.

FIRST, Ruth
    The Barrel of a Gun: political power in Africa and the
    coup d'etat   (London: Allen Lane, The Penguin Press,
    1970)   513 pp.
    Bibliography.

Case studies of Sudan, Nigeria and Ghana. Interested in
the way army interventions reveal nature of political
power and its areas of failure in Africa.

GRUNDY, Kenneth
    Conflicting Images of the Military in Africa   (Nairobi:
    East Africa Publishing House, 1968)   33 pp.

Monograph discusses positive and negative aspects of
military's role and image. Appendix has country-by-
country listing of all major coups, secessions or mutin-
ies that involved the military or portions of the military.

GUTTERIDGE, W.F.
    The Military in African Politics   (London: Methuen & Co.
    Ltd., 1969)   166 pp.
    Bibliography.

Combines historical approach with political analysis.
Provides introduction to assessing origin and nature of
trend towards military intervention in Africa. Studies
examples in Francophone Africa, Nigeria and Ghana.

GUTTERIDGE, W.F.
>   Military Regimes in Africa   (London: Methuen & Co., Ltd.,
>   1975)   189 pp.
>   Bibliography.
>
>   Sequel to The Military in African Politics (1969).
>   Emphasizes performance of military in power, rather than
>   military seizure of power. Uses six country case stud-
>   ies taken from last decade: Ghana, Dahomey, Nigeria,
>   Zaire, Uganda, Sudan.

HACHTEN, William A.
>   Muffled Drums: the news media in Africa   (Iowa: Iowa
>   State University Press, 1971)   314 pp.
>   Bibliography.
>
>   Especially interesting for discussion of government in-
>   volvement in news media and aspects of political commun-
>   ication; includes a number of comparative case studies
>   of country news media systems -- show how local politi-
>   cal, social and economic factors shape media system of
>   individual country.

HODGKIN, Thomas
>   African Political Parties   (Harmondsworth, Middlesex:
>   Penguin Books, 1961)   217 pp.
>   Bibliography.
>
>   Classic study of political parties in African context:
>   origins, types, organization, objectives, activities.
>   Appendix gives details of main parties operating during
>   1945-60, by country.

JANOWITZ, Morris
>   The Military in the Political Development of New Nations
>   (Chicago: University of Chicago Press, 1967)   134 pp.
>
>   Comparative analysis of military in Africa and Asia;
>   finds that ability of military to intervene in politics
>   comes from their organizational resources, their pro-
>   fessional commitments and their sense of national iden-
>   tity; finds that they are limited by lack of political
>   skill and inability to mobilize mass support. Book
>   provides framework for further investigations.

JOHNSON, John J., ed.
>   The Role of the Military in Underdeveloped Countries
>   (Princeton, N.J.: Princeton University Press, 1962)
>   423 pp.
>
>   Articles basically concerned with civil-military rela-

tions and with discerning why military governments in
some countries have promoted national development and
why others have been only a retarding influence. Articles cover examples from all regions, providing comparative analysis.

JULY, Robert W.
The Origins of Modern African Thought: its development
in West Africa during the 19th and 20th centuries
(London: Faber & Faber, 1968)   512 pp.
Bibliography.

Author explores impact made by intrusion of Western sci-
entific-technological revolution into Africa (does not
treat second important influence: Islam); considers both
impact on nationalist thought and on confrontation between two ways of life.

KLINGHOFFER, Arthur Jay
Soviet Perspectives on African Socialism (Rutherford:
Fairleigh Dickinson University Press, 1969)   276 pp.
Bibliography.

Covers Khruschev period (1955-64) and is geographically
limited to sub-Saharan Africa. Covers Soviet view of
contemporary African socialism as an ideology and in its
possible application to a class struggle in African society (roles of classes) and Soviet view of Africa's
future transition to scientific socialism.

LAVROFF, Dmitri G.
Les Partis Politiques en Afrique Noire (Paris: Presses
Universitaires de France, 1970)   124 pp.
Bibliography.

Considers formation of political parties, establishment
of one-party states and therein, place of political
party in political system as a whole; concludes with
view of future and suggests that role of political party
may be superceded by army.

LEE, John Michael
African Armies and Civil Order (Institute of Strategic
Studies; London: Chatto & Windus, 1969)   198 pp.
Bibliography.

Studies existence or nonexistence of common language of
politics in new state which may lead to either civil
order or to possibilities of military intervention; discusses role of military in terms of newly independent

societies and problems of new political functions to be
performed; provides unusual material on the ethnic composition of army.

LEFEVER, Ernest W.
Spear and Scepter: army, police, and politics in tropical Africa (Washington, D.C.: The Brookings Institution, 1970)   251 pp.
Bibliography.

Analyzes role of military and police in state-building;
gives primary attention to Ghana, Zaire, Ethiopia.
Study not confined to unconstitutional interventions in
politics, but covers wide range of relations between
military power and political authority.

LEVINE, Victor T.
Political Leadership in Africa (Stanford, Calif.: The
Hoover Institution, 1967)   114 pp.

Study of elites, based on interviews/questionnaires.
Author focuses on problems of leadership transition and
generational conflict, i.e. between elder statesmen who
fought against colonialism, founded political parties
and formed nationalist ideologies, and younger men who
have attained political leadership since independence
and whose goals relate more to post-independence situation (economic development, establishment of effective
central government, etc.).

LITTLE, Kenneth
West African Urbanization: a study of voluntary associ-
ations in social change (London: Cambridge University
Press, 1965)
Bibliography.

Suggests that voluntary associations provide system of
relationships which link old with new structures in
society; takes functional approach to role of voluntary
associations, shows their relation to emerging class
structure. Discusses adaptation and integration effects
as applied to such groups as migrant workers, younger
men, women, etc.

LLOYD, Peter C.
Classes, Crises and Coups: themes in the sociology of
developing countries (London: MacGibbon & Kee, 1971)
224 pp.
Bibliography.

Emphasis on sociological approach but highly relevant to
politics. Discusses variables which directly affect
socio-political outcome in ldc's; compares these variables in context of African, Asian and Latin American
countries in trying to understand relationships between
them. Variables include: nature of rural demands and
form of rural protest; poverty and unemployment in cities, migrants' image of their society, associations
through which they pursue their goals; characteristics
of dominant elite and extent/nature of intra-elite com-
petition for power.

LLOYD, Peter C., ed.
The New Elites of Tropical Africa (International African Institute; Oxford: Oxford University Press, 1966)
390 pp.

Studies presented at Sixth International African Seminar
at University of Ibadan, Nigeria, in July 1964. Include
comprehensive introduction by Lloyd: his sociological
approach to analysis portrays characteristics and variations of contemporary elites in Africa, their development in relation to educational advance, their part in
traditional and modern associations, evidence for
achievement motivation and their relations with unedu-
cated.

LYND, G.E.
The Politics of African Trade Unionism (New York:
Praeger, 1968) 198 pp.
Bibliography.

Centres on problems and attitudes of African labour
leaders, their involvement in domestic politics, and
their responses to Western and other international over-
tures. Describes position of unions in one-party states
of Ghana, Kenya, Tanzania and of unions in Swaziland
and Nigeria, so-called democratically-oriented states.

MINER, Horace, ed.
The City in Modern Africa (New York: Praeger, 1967;
London: Pall Mall Press, 1967) 364 pp.
Bibliography.

Series of papers designed to set out some aspects of
'new' African cities and to highlight possibilities for
research. Papers study variety of subjects from point
of view of social science disciplines: modernization,
urbanization and economic growth, racial pluralism,

community political structure, family relationships, etc.

MAZRUI, Ali A., and R.I. ROTBERG, eds.
Protest and Power in Black Africa (New York: Oxford University Press, 1970)   1,274 pp.
Bibliography.

Comprehensive anthology dealing with various forms of resistance to colonization and to post-colonial rule. Book has three major themes: dissent, diversity, rein- tegration -- covers resistance to conquest, rebellion against alien rule, religious expressions of discontent, pressure groups/political parties, economic expression of discontent, literary protest, revolutions and coups in post-independence period, sovereignty and diplomacy.

MAZRUI, Ali A.
Towards a Pax Africana: a study of ideology and ambition (London: Weidenfeld & Nicolson, 1967)   287 pp.

Author is well-known African scholar, theorist. Attempt to describe, interpret and evaluate African political thought, both on basis of what is said by African lead- ers and of their behaviour and emotional orientation in specific situations; divided into two main sections: ideology and identity, and dilemmas of statehood. Most ideas discussed have international implications.

MAZRUI, Ali A.
Violence and Thought: essays on social tensions in Africa (London: Longmans, Green & Co., Ltd., 1969) 351 pp.

Includes some articles previously published in journals. From political scientist's perspective, attempts to elucidate areas of contact between phenomena of viol- ence, symbols of power in society, process of national development and instincts of man in society. First articles on military and violence are slightly repiti- tious; has interesting discussion of plural societies and conflict resolution. Study focuses on Africa, but has wider theoretical application.

MEYNAUD, Jean, and Anissa SALAY-BEY
Trade Unionism in Africa: a study of its growth and orientation (London: Methuen & Co., 1967)   242 pp.
Bibliography.

Includes useful documentary annexes. Analyzes stages

and means of growth of African trade unionism from its
origins until mid-1962. Especially tries to situate
unions in their relations with government policies; discusses role of unions during colonial period and struggle for independence, their links with Central Europeans, their actual mission in organization of African
workers, etc.

NOVEMBER, Andras
      L'Evolution du Mouvement Syndical en Afrique Occidentale
      (Institut Africain de Geneve; Paris: Mouton, 1965)
      282 pp.
      Bibliography (French and English sources).

      Studies relations between trade unionism and politics
      in countries of West Africa (both former French and
      English colonies); studies French and English influence
      and relation between unions and struggles for indepen-
      dence. Also deals with international and pan-African
      trade union movements.

OLORUNSOLA, Victor, ed.
      The Politics of Cultural Sub-Nationalism in Africa
      (Garden City, N.Y.: Doubleday & Co., 1972)   340 pp.

      Case studies of Nigeria, Uganda, Sierra Leone, Congo-
      Kinshasa, Kenya. Each chapter includes useful tables
      regarding ethnic composition of society and relevant
      indices of political attitudes, etc. Studies problems
      of integrating sub-national groups into nation-state.

ONUOHA, Father Bede
      The Elements of African Socialism   (London: Andre
      Deutsch, 1965)   139 pp.
      Bibliography.

      Nigerian priest's interpretation of African socialism in
      light of his Catholic education/bias; places emphasis on
      communitarism. Author takes middle-of-the-road position
      rejecting both laissez-faire capitalism and Marxist
      socialism.

SIGMUND, P., ed.
      Ideologies of Developing Nations   (New York: Praeger,
      1967)   Revised edition.   428 pp.
      Bibliography.

      Anthology of political theories and ideologies of lead-
      ers of developing nations: based on excerpts from their
      writings and speeches. Includes chapters on OAU, OCAM,

Sekou Toure, Madeira Keita, L.S. Senghor, Kwame Nkrumah, J.A. Ankrah, Kenyatta, Julius Nyerere, plus sections on other geographical regions.

SKURNIK, W.A.E., ed.
   African Political Thought: Lumumba, Nkrumah, and Toure (Denver: Graduate School of International Studies, University of Denver, 1968)   147 pp.

   Three essays comparing political thought of 'radical' African leaders who emerged under three different colonial powers. Concerned mainly with traditional spheres of political thought: nature and purpose of historical forces, bases of political legitimacy, role of decision-makers, relations between man and society. Takes critical approach, examining influence of environmental and cultural factors.

THOMAS, L.V.
   Le Socialisme et L'Afrique, Two Volumes (Paris: Le Livre Africain, 1966)   203 pp. & 298 pp.

   Volume One is essay on African socialism treating such issues as its place in socialist thought generally, its relation to religion in Africa, and its place in traditional and modern Africa. Volume Two discusses socialist ideology and its effect on African paths to development; in particular, refers to ideology of Senegalese leaders, of other francophone leaders, of anglophone leaders and of leaders in white Africa (including Arab).

VAN DOORN, Jacques, ed.
   Armed Forces and Society: sociological essays   (Paris: Mouton, 1968)   386 pp.

   Although labelled as sociology, this is also of great interest to political scientists. Comparative sociology of military institutions: provides comparisons among armies of both developed and developing countries (especially interested in aspects of professionalism/ militarism and effects on behaviour of military establishment in different contexts).

WELCH, Claude E., Jr., ed.
   Soldier and State in Africa: a comparative analysis of military intervention and political change   (Evanston, Ill.: Northwestern University Press, 1970)   320 pp. Bibliography.

Analyzes factors leading to military involvement in politics and impact of military-based rule upon individual
African states. Appendix provides chronological pre-
sentation by country of violence and military involvement in politics from independence through 1968.

WORSLEY, Peter
   The Third World (London: Weidenfeld & Nicolson, 1971)
   373 pp.
   Bibliography.

   Discusses processes of socio-political change and analyzes such factors as nationalism, populism, appeal of
   communism, neutralism, and supra-national movements.
   Assesses continuing pressures toward 'revolution' and
   efforts to contain it.

D. BIOGRAPHIES, MEMOIRS, SPEECHES, WRITINGS
BY POLITICAL LEADERS

BUSIA, K.A.
   Africa in Search of Democracy (London: Routledge &
   Kegan Paul, 1967)   189 pp.

   Written by leader of Ghana parliamentary opposition and
   of United Party which, opposed Nkrumah, while in exile.
   Basically an attempt to establish that African heritage
   (political and social) has prepared the way for democracy in African nations, and that democracy is proper
   course.

EMERSON, Rupert, and Martin KILSON, eds.
   The Political Awakening of Africa (Englewood Cliffs,
   N.J.: Prentice-Hall, 1965)   175 pp.
   Bibliography.

   Collection of passages by African leaders and intellectuals on self-identity in African development, ideas
   and context of African nationalism, policies and methods
   of African political parties, and inter-African problems
   and Pan-Africanism.

FRIEDLAND, W., and C. ROSBERG, eds.
   African Socialism (Hoover Institution; Stanford, Calif:
   Stanford University Press, 1964)   313 pp.

   Attempt to define African socialism as an ideology and
   to gauge its impact on action in independent states of
   Africa, with case studies of Ghana, Guinea, Mali,
   Senegal, Tanzania. Includes series of excerpts from

writings of African leaders who are proponents of
African socialism.

MINOGUE, Martin, and Judith MOLLOY, eds.
   African Aims and Attitudes: selected documents (London:
   Cambridge University Press, 1974)   400 pp.
   Bibliography.

   Provides excerpts from writings and speeches of African
   leaders and intellectuals, aimed at acquainting students with their political attitudes and objectives.
   Covers subjects of colonialism and decolonization, nation-building, Pan-Africanism, current issues, political
   attitudes of military.

PADMORE, George
   Pan-Africanism or Communism: the coming struggle for
   Africa (London: Dennis Dobson, 1956; Garden City, N.Y.:
   Doubleday, 1971)   463 pp.

   Attempts to explain realistically the relationship between communism and African, West Indian and American
   Negro mass movements and to discredit argument that
   African nationalist movements were communist-inspired.
   Examines back-to-Africa movements, Garveyism, Pan-Africanism; compares different colonial policies and their
   effects/results vis-a-vis type of nationalist movement.

SEGAL, Ronald
   African Profiles (Harmondsworth, Middlesex: Penguin
   African Library, Penguin Books, 1962)   352 pp.

   Many of biographies are based on accounts originally
   published in Political Africa (1961) by Segal. African
   Profiles provides biographical sketches of contemporary
   African leaders of early 1960s and provides guide to
   more general political situation in each country.

TAYLOR, Sidney, ed.
   The New Africans (New York: Putnam, 1967; London: Paul
   Hamlyn, 1967)   504 pp.

   Written by correspondents of Reuters news agency.
   Guide to contemporary history of emergent Africa and its
   leaders. Provides brief description of each country
   and political background of major political figures.

VAN RENSBURG, A.P.J.
   Contemporary Leaders of Africa (Cape Town/Pretoria:
   HAUM, 1975)   529 pp.

Series of essays describing political careers and personalities of African leaders. Although published in
South Africa, essays are objective as well as extremely
informative, not only regarding the individual leaders
but also their countries.

E. EXTERNAL RELATIONS: INTERNATIONAL POLITICS WHOSE CONCERN
IS PRIMARILY AFRICAN AND ARAB STATES

American Society of African Culture, eds.
Pan-Africanism Reconsidered (Berkeley/Los Angeles:
University of California Press, 1962) 377 pp.

Conference papers from Third Annual Conference of AMSAC
(1960). Covers wide range of subjects including politics, economics, education, social thought, art, culture, etc. Of particular interest are chapters on Pan-
Africanism (gives historical/contemporary survey) and on
politics (written largely by Apter and Coleman).

BRZEZINSKI, Zbigniew, ed.
Africa and the Communist World (Stanford, Calif.:
Stanford University Press, 1964; London: Oxford Univer-
sity Press, 1964) 272 pp.

Examines communist policies toward Africa; analyzes
programmes adopted by various communist states to establish their influence in Africa, but does not assess
degree of penetration; compares and contrasts different
approaches of various communist countries.

CERVENKA, Zdenek
The Organization of African Unity and Its Charter
(London: C. Hurst & Co., 1969) Second edition. 253 pp.

Includes political and legal analysis of Charter, discussion of organs for peaceful settlement of disputes
within OAU, relations between OAU and UN, relations between OAU and regional political groups in Africa.
Also includes several case studies plus documents.

COHN, Helen Desfosses
Soviet Policy Toward Black Africa: the focus on nation-
al integration (New York: Praeger, 1972) 316 pp.
Bibliography.

Analyzes Soviet theories regarding nation-building process in black Africa, especially evolution of Soviet
views regarding applicability of political/economic
aspects of Soviet integration model. Argues that

during Brezhnev-Kosygin regime, model has become flexi-
ble; Soviets admit that installation of socialist systems in Africa will be slow process. Bibliography is
valuable for its detailed listing of modern Russian
books and articles.

DECRAENE, Philippe
    Le Panafricanisme (Paris: Presses Universitaires de
    France, 1964)   128 pp.
    Bibliography.

    Traces history of Pan-Africanism movement from beginning
    of 20th century. Studies it in context of independence
    movements in Africa and then of attempts at regional
    grouping. Considers obstacles found both in African
    society itself and in international community.

DIA, Mamadou
    The African Nations and World Solidarity (London: Thames
    and Hudson, 1962)   145 pp.

    Translated from French edition published in 1960.
    Author is socialist but argues against communism (Soviet
    type) which promulgates another sort of imperialism al-
    though not direct colonialism. Supports Francois Per-
    roux's theory of mutual development and argues for sol-
    idarity among African nations. Admits mistakes made by
    his government (he served as prime minister of Senegal)
    which led to failure of Mali federation.

DUMOGA, John
    Africa Between East and West (London: Bodley Head,
    1969)   142 pp.

    Examines problems in post-independence Africa related to
    nationalism, ideological struggle between proponents of
    East and West for control of Africa, and the effects of
    this struggle on policies of some African countries
    (questions of democracy, unity, socialism, etc.). Tries
    to suggest some solutions and stresses responsibility of
    African leaders.

EMERSON, Rupert
    Africa and United States Policy (Englewood Cliffs, N.J.
    :Prentice-Hall, 1967)   117 pp.
    Bibliography.

    One of a series on America's role in world affairs.
    Discusses post-war relations between US and Africa, ex-
    tent of American interests (political and economic) in

Africa; case studies of 'trouble areas' like Congo,
Portuguese colonies (former), Rhodesia, South Africa.

GEISS, Imanuel
    The Pan-African Movement   (London: Methuen & Co., Ltd.,
    1974)   575 pp.
    Bibliography.

    First published in German in 1968. Social/intellectual
    history based on original research, dealing largely
    with period up to 1945. Views Pan-Africanism as reac-
    tion of modernized intellectual elites (African and
    Afro-American) to white (European and American) supre-
    macy either in form of slavery, racial discrimination or
    colonial rule. Also, later seen as attempt to achieve
    some form of unity on African continent.

HAMRELL, Sven, and Carl Gosta WIDSTRAND, eds.
    The Soviet Bloc, China and Africa   (Uppsala: Scandinav-
    ian Institute of African Studies, 1964)   173 pp.

    Conference papers presented in November 1963, related
    to two objectives: to elucidate policy of Soviet bloc
    and China towards Africa against background of old con-
    flict between Pan-Africanism and communism, and to
    assess degree of actual and potential communist influ-
    ence in Africa and repercussions of Sino-Soviet dispute
    in this context.

HAZLEWOOD, Arthur, ed.
    African Integration and Disintegration: case studies in
    economic and political union   (London: Oxford University
    Press, 1967)   414 pp.
    Bibliography.

    Following editor's introduction, articles discuss case
    studies of various types of integration attempts: econ-
    omic unions, political unions, Pan-Africanism.

LARKIN, Bruce D.
    China and Africa 1949-1970   (Berkeley/Los Angeles:
    University of California Press, 1971)   268 pp.
    Bibliography.

    Argues that impetus for much of China's present activi-
    ty is commitment to world revolution. Studies state-
    ments and actions of CCP (China) in order to further
    discern goals; distinguishes between long- vs short-
    term goals and between policies which have domestic vs
    foreign ends.

LEGUM, Colin
Pan-Africanism: a short political guide   (London: Pall
Mall Press, 1965)   Revised edition.   326 pp.

Covers period between 1900-1964; discusses beginnings of
the movement in 'Diaspora', the 'back-to-Africa' campaign, and finally the contemporary African version of
Pan-Africanism and its implications for politics. Includes 150 pp. of appendices with texts of many important documents related to Pan-Africanism.

LEGVOLD, Robert
Soviet Policy in West Africa   (Cambridge, Mass.: Har-
vard University Press, 1970)   372 pp.
Bibliography.

Studies Soviet foreign policy towards Guinea, Ghana,
Ivory Coast, Mali, Nigeria, Senegal - these six represent in their differing foreign and domestic attitudes
the full spectrum of countries which Soviet Union has
dealt with in black Africa. Author is especially concerned with Soviets' changing objectives over the period and relation between economic and political objectives.

McKAY, Vernon, ed.
African Diplomacy: studies in the determinants of foreign policy   (School of Advanced International Studies,
Johns Hopkins University; London: Pall Mall Press,
1966)   210 pp.

Essays by well-known Africanists: try to analyze factors that shape foreign relations and foreign policies
of African states. Essays take interdisciplinary approach and deal with such topics as international conflict patterns, national interest and ideology, internal
and external economic forces, military factors, and
political and cultural factors. Also pinpoint problems
for further research.

MAZRUI, Ali A.
The Anglo-African Commonwealth: political friction and
cultural fusion   (Oxford: Pergamon Press, Ltd., 1967)
163 pp.

Discusses evolution of Africa's role within Commonwealth
including aspects of history and politics, culture and
thought. Appendices are documents related to above
subjects. Emphasizes changing balance of racial composition in Commonwealth; attempts to assess nature of

Commonwealth in general.

NIELSEN, Waldemar A.
The Great Powers and Africa (for the Council on Foreign
Relations; London: Pall Mall Press, 1969)   431 pp.

Puts US policy in context of policies pursued by other
great powers (Europe, communist powers). Argues that
US policies towards Africa had stagnated in post-war
period, that American policy was reactive rather than
active and pragmatic rather than doctrinaire, and that
policies were often shaped by events outside Africa itself. Concludes with policy recommendations for future.

RIVKIN, Arnold
The African Presence in World Affairs (New York: Free
Press of Glencoe, 1963)   304 pp.

Relates national development objectives/policies in
African states to role of Africa in world affairs.
However, book is outdated in sense that nature of international relations has changed considerably since 1963;
book is useful, then, in presenting early foreign policies of African states but cannot be applied to current
policies.

THIAM, Doudou
The Foreign Policy of African States: ideological bases,
present realities, future prospects (London: J.M. Dent
& Sons, Ltd., 1965)   134 pp.

Translated from French edition. Author is foreign minister of Senegal. Discusses internal and external factors which affect policies of African nations, some of
which they have in common; studies nationalism and socialism as ideological bases of international policies;
considers international policy in practice, based on his
experience. Advocates non-alignment.

THOMPSON, Vincent Bakpetu
Africa and Unity: the evolution of Pan-Africanism
(London: Longmans, Green & Co., Ltd., 1969)   412 pp.
Bibliography.

Analyzes activities of two phases in evolution of Pan-
Africanism: 1900-45 realm of ideas; after 1945, mili-
tancy and struggles for independence. Provides historical justification and explanation for protest activity
that eventually led to Pan-Africanism. Discusses formation of OAU and modern problems of unity. Appendices.

TOUVAL, Saadia
  The Boundary Politics of Independent Africa (Cambridge,
  Mass.: Harvard University Press, 1972)   334 pp.

  Argues that principal factors determining policies of
  states on boundary problems are not geographical but
  political, and as political have direct relation to process of state-building. Presents background of boundary
  politics and reviews instruments of policy.

WALLERSTEIN, Immanuel
  Africa: the politics of unity (London: Pall Mall Press,
  1967)   274 pp.

  This book is sequel to Wallerstein's Africa: the politics of independence (1961). Interprets political development in Africa (1957-65) in light of movement
  towards African unity. Argues that this movement was
  strongest indigenous force in Africa during this period
  although it did not achieve all of its objectives.

WEINSTEIN, Warren, ed.
  Chinese and Soviet Aid to Africa   (New York: Praeger,
  1975)   290 pp.

  Compares Chinese and Soviet aid to Africa in its economic and political aspects during the period since 1960.
  Includes interesting case studies of Tanzam Railway,
  Ghana, Guinea, Nigeria, Somalia, and of aid to African
  liberation movements. Provides useful data on aid
  flows.

WODIE, Francis
  Les Institutions Regionales en Afrique Occidentale et
  Centrale (Librairie Generale de Droit et de Jurispru-
  dence; Paris: R. Pichon et R. Durand-Auzias, 1970)
  274 pp.
  Bibliography.

  Presents overview of regional organizations, both general ones and smaller, limited organizations in a variety of spheres; demonstrates that the idea of African
  unity, sometimes uncertain in political domain, leads
  to interesting application in sectors where politics
  play a secondary role.

WORONOFF, Jon
  Organizing African Unity (Metuchen, N.J.: The Scare-
  crow Press, Inc., 1970)   703 pp.
  Bibliography.

Introduction to study of Pan-Africanism, focuses mainly
on OAU and its role in various African conflicts and
crises.

ZARTMAN, I. William
International Relations in the New Africa (Englewood
Cliffs, N.J.: Prentice-Hall, 1966)   175 pp.

Study is diplomatic history emphasizing three foreign
policy goals: independence, unity and development.
Examines development of foreign relations among new
states of North and West Africa between 1956-65; tries
to test general theories of international relations on
new area of study. Also studies foreign relations that
existed before independent states were created.

CENTRAL AFRICA

A. POLITICAL HISTORY

DE DREUX-BREZE, Joachim
Le Probleme du Regroupement en Afrique Equatoriale - du
regime colonial a l'Union Douaniere et Economique de
l'Afrique Centrale (Librairie Generale de Droit et de
Jurisprudence; Paris: R. Pichon et R. Durand-Auzias,
1968) 211 pp.
Bibliography.

Studies evolution of administration and politics in
French Equatorial Africa with reference to structure of
this system, i.e., as an administrative totality during
colonial period, then as separate nation-states; finally
studies movements towards regrouping independent countries in various forms and levels of association.

THOMPSON, Virginia, and Richard ADLOFF
The Emerging States of French Equatorial Africa (Stan-
ford, Calif.: Stanford University Press, 1960) 595 pp.
Bibliography.

This book was probably the authoritative study of its
period; it covers an area not often written of by Eng-
lish-speaking academics. Part I provides survey of
various political/economic aspects of federation:
Afrique Equatoriale Francaise (AEF). Part II treats
each territory separately with regard to its politics
and economics (Gabon, Central African Republic, Chad,
Republic of the Congo).

1. Central African Republic

KALCK, Pierre
Central African Republic: a failure in decolonization
(London: Pall Mall Press, 1971) 206 pp.
Bibliography.

Traces political development of CAR from colonial period until ten years after independence. Concludes that
CAR has not achieved a viable political system which is
capable of promoting political/economic development.

2. Chad

LE CORNEC, Jacques

31

Histoire Politique du Tchad, de 1900 a 1962 (Librairie Generale de Droit et de Jurisprudence; Paris: R. Pichon et R. Durand-Auzias, 1963)   374 pp.
Bibliography.

Written by former French administrator in Africa. On the whole, seems to be comprehensive study of evolution of political system, taking account of traditional/modern conflicts, ethnic differences, etc. Does not treat sufficiently relationship with France after independence which has been called 'neo-colonialist' or 'imperialist' by other authors. Main emphasis is on 'la chefferie' institution and how it has been assimilated/integrated into modern system.

3. Republic of the Congo (Brazzaville)

GAUZE, Rene
> The Politics of Congo-Brazzaville (Stanford, Calif.: Hoover Institution Press, 1973)   283 pp.
> Bibliography.

Translated, edited and supplemented by V. Thompson and R. Adloff. Author was in French colonial service and some of his judgments of Congolese politicians are controversial. Gauze covers period 1945-61; editors bring it up to 1972. Emphasizes impact of tribal conflicts on political evolution; discusses role of Fulbert Youlou, Congo's first president.

WAGRET, Jean-Michel
> Histoire et Sociologie Politique de la Republique du Congo (Brazzaville) (Librairie Generale de Droit et de Jurisprudence; Paris: R. Pichon et R. Durand-Auzias, 1963)   247 pp.
> Bibliography.

First section discusses political history beginning in colonial period around 1875; second section describes societal structures, political parties and other political forces.

WOUNGLY-MASSAGA
> La Revolution au Congo: contribution a l'etude des problemes politiques d'Afrique centrale (Paris: Francois Maspero, 1974)   182 pp.

From socialist and Pan-Africanist perspective, analyzes political history of Congo: traces history of ancient Kingdom of Congo (14th-15th centruies) up to dictator-

ship of Youlou which inspired revolutionary period.
Expresses solidarity between UPC (Cameroon) and revolution in Congo.

4. Gabon

WEINSTEIN, Brian
    Gabon: nation-building on the Ogooue   (Cambridge, Mass.:
    MIT Press, 1966)   287 pp.
    Bibliography.

    Studies interaction between Fang and French, and in gen-
    eral, colonial experience which led to nationalism; con-
    siders aspects of national consolidation through shared
    experience and through conscious decision-making. Book's
    methodology based on specific concept of nation-building
    and need for nations.

5. Rwanda and Burundi

LEMARCHAND, Rene
    Rwanda and Burundi   (London: Pall Mall Press, 1970)
    562 pp.
    Bibliography.

    The only major study published in English. Treats each
    country separately in regard to recent political devel-
    opments because each state has exhibited radically dif-
    ferent pattern of evolution: argues that Rwanda experi-
    enced genuine revolutionary change (total reversal in
    dominant political class) while Burundi experienced only
    process of evolution.

MAIRIEU, Baudouin Paternostre de la
    Le Rwanda: son effort de developpement   (Brussels:
    Editions A. de Boeck, 1972; Kigali: Editions Rwandaises,
    1972)   413 pp.
    Bibliography.

    Part I describes Rwanda's political history up to inde-
    pendence; Part II deals with post-independence period
    and socio-political change moving towards democratic
    development of political and economic system.

6. Zaire

ANSTEY, Roger
    King Leopold's Legacy: the Congo under Belgian rule
    1908-1960 (Institute of Race Relations; London: Oxford
    University Press, 1966)   293 pp.

Bibliography.

Discusses reasons behind Belgian presence in Congo, what goals were, what impact of presence was. Considers effects of pressures imposed by colonial administration, effects of process of economic growth, urbanization and education, and effects of creation of self-conscious elite (evolues) leading to protest and revolt. Argues that Belgians lacked any national purpose for Congo.

GERARD-LIBOIS, Jules
Katanga Secession (Madison: University of Wisconsin Press, 1966) 377 pp.

Analyzes events which led to secession movement in Katanga, as led by Moise Tshombe. Includes appendices of relevant documents.

HOSKYNS, Catherine
The Congo Since Independence: January 1960 - December 1961 (Royal Institute of International Affairs; London: Oxford University Press, 1965) 518 pp.
Bibliography.

Aim was to relate internal and external aspects of Congo crisis and to show at each stage how events outside Congo reacted on those inside and vice-versa.

LEMARCHAND, Rene
Political Awakening in the Belgian Congo (Berkeley/Los Angeles: University of California Press, 1964) 357 pp.

Analyzes particular Congolese experience of Belgian colonial rule and development of Congolese political groups and parties in nationalist movement. Main objective is to analyze causes of political fragmentation in Congolese politics.

WEISS, Herbert F.
Political Protest in the Congo: the Parti Solidaire Africain during the independence struggle (Princeton, N.J.: Princeton University Press, 1967) 362 pp.
Bibliography.

Studies evolution of political parties in Congo and their functional problems; then focuses on PSA, describing its history and leadership; finally, discusses rural radicalism and its relation to party. In particular, argues that rural masses were more radicalized than party leadership because of colonial experience, but says that eventually most of Congo did manifest revolutionary protest.

YOUNG, M. Crawford
    Politics in the Congo: decolonization and independence
    (Princeton, N.J.: Princeton University Press, 1965)
    659 pp.

    Examines political history since World War II in so far
    as it helps to explain political system since 1960;
    deals with Belgian effort to engineer Congo and anal-
    yzes Congolese response to colonialism; concludes by
    analyzing trends and forces emerging from 1960-1 crisis.

B. POLITICAL SYSTEMS, GOVERNMENT

1. Central African Republic

KALCK, Pierre
    La Republique Centrafricaine (Encyclopedie Politique et
    Constitutionnelle, Institut International d'Administra-
    tion Publique; Paris: Editions Berger-Levrault, 1971)
    51 pp.
    Bibliography.

    Outlines Central African society, political evolution
    and contemporary political system. Appendices with
    texts of constitutional acts.

2. Chad

GONIDEC, P.F.
    La Republique du Tchad (Encyclopedie Politique et Con-
    stitutionnelle, Institut International d'Administration
    Publique; Paris: Editions Berger-Levrault, 1971) 79 pp.
    Bibliography.

    Outlines Chad society, political evolution to 1962 and
    political forces acting in system today (single party,
    traditional chiefs, trade unionism).

5. Rwanda and Burundi

MPOZAGARA, Gabriel
    La Republique du Burundi (Encyclopedie Politique et
    Constitutionnelle, Institut International d'Administra-
    tion Publique; Paris: Editions Berger-Levrault, 1971)
    71 pp.
    Bibliography.

    Describes geographical, demographic, economic, social
    and cultural context of Burundi political system;

briefly considers periods as mandate and trust territory of UN and Belgium until independence; presents
political forces (parties, youth movement, unions); describes political life since independence including
such issues as primacy of party, return to royal autocracy, republican period, problem of legitimacy and man-
agement of power. Concludes with text of party charter
and other documents.

NSANZE, Terence
L'Edification de la Republique du Burundi au Carrefour
de l'Afrique (Brussels: Editions Remarques Africaines,
Collection 'Etudes Africaines', No. 15, 1970)   156 pp.
Bibliography.

Author was head of Burundi mission to UN, then ambassador to Washington and Ottawa. Presents brief historical
/ethnical background, including introduction to political parties; analyzes institution of royal dynasty as
source of political power; argues that decision of roy-
alty to maintain its power by return to despotic authority brought about final end to royal presence in political scene. Describes creation of Burundi Republic in
1966; poses issues of tribal conflicts vs nation, relations with Belgium, and role of intelligentsia in modernization process.

VANDERLINDEN, Jacques
La Republique Rwandaise (Encyclopedie Politique et Con-
stitutionnelle, Institut International d'Administration
Publique; Paris: Editions Berger-Levrault, 1970)   63 pp.
Bibliography.

Discusses demographic, economic, cultural and social
factors in Rwanda society; outlines political and constitutional evolution from monarchy to colonial period;
describes current political regime, especially four
issues: as symbol of abolition of past, religious anti-
communist republic, multipartyism of law and single par-
tyism in reality, separation of powers in cooperation.
Concludes with texts of constitution and other documents.

6. Zaire

MPINGA-KASENDA
L'Administration Publique du Zaire   (Paris: Editions A.
Pedone, 1973)   316 pp.
Bibliography.

Studies impact of socio-political milieu on structure

and functioning of public administration; argues that
it must also be adapted from inherited forms to better
suit environment of independent African state.

VIEUX, Serge A.
    L'Administration Zairoise (Encyclopedie Administrative,
    Institut International d'Administration Publique; Paris:
    Editions Berger-Levrault, 1974)   96 pp.
    Bibliography.

    Outlines structures and functions of Zaire's administra-
    tion, institutional origins and characteristics of ad-
    ministration, personnel and programmes and coordination
    of administrative action.

WILLAME, Jean-Claude
    Patrimonialism and Political Change in the Congo (Stan-
    ford, Calif.: Stanford University Press, 1972)   223 pp.
    Bibliography.

    Uses 'patrimonialism' as system-related concept to ana-
    lyze Congolese political experience in three components:
    appropriation of public offices as elites' prime source
    of status, prestige and reward; political and territor-
    ial fragmentation through development of relationships
    based on primordial and personal loyalties; use of pri-
    vate armies, militias and mercenaries as chief instru-
    ments of rule.

D. BIOGRAPHIES, MEMOIRS, SPEECHES, WRITINGS
BY POLITICAL LEADERS

6. Zaire

ARTIGUE, Pierre
    Qui Sont Les Leaders Congolais? (Brussels: Editions
    Europe-Afrique, 1960)   139 pp.

    Provides biographical sketches of 200 most prominent
    Congolese between 1956-60; in second part, lists and
    describes parties, groups, associations cited in bio-
    graphies; in third part, provides composition of trans-
    ition institutions created following Round Table Confer-
    ence of February 1960.

CHOME, Jules
    L'Ascension de Mobutu (Brussels: Editions Complexes,
    1974)   198 pp.

    Analyzes Mobutu's rise to power, his background and
    his personality and views. Author emphasizes under-

handed tactics of Mobutu and his early links with such
groups as Belgian secret police and CIA; accuses
Mobutu of presiding over repressive dictatorship.

COLVIN, Ian
    The Rise and Fall of Moise Tshombe   (London: Leslie
    Frewin, 1968)   263 pp.
    Bibliography.

    Sympathetic biography of Moise Tshombe concentrates on
    period of Congo crisis and on Tshombe's leadership of
    Katangans. Written in rather journalistic manner, but
    author apparently obtained much source material from
    Tshombe himself and others directly involved.

KANZA, Thomas
    Conflict in the Congo   (Penguin African Library; Har-
    mondsworth, Middlesex: Penguin Books, 1972)   346 pp.

    Kanza was friend of Lumumba and minister in his govern-
    ment. Traces history of Lumumba's part in liberation
    of Congo and in struggle to create viable government;
    discusses Belgian attempts to sabotage newly independ-
    ent country.

LUMUMBA, Patrice
    Congo My Country   (London: Pall Mall Press, 1962) 195
    pp.

    Originally published in French: Le Congo - Terre d'Ave-
    nir - Est-il Menace? (1961). This edition has introduc-
    tion by Colin Legum who puts book in context of Lumum-
    ba's actual role in Congo. Book was written by Lumumba
    in 1956-7. Provides political record of Lumumba's de-
    velopment, his ideas, and provides insight into atti-
    tudes and feelings of Congolese elite towards Belgian
    rule.

NKRUMAH, Kwame
    Challenge of the Congo   (London: Thomas Nelson & Sons,
    Ltd., 1967)   304 pp.
    Bibliography.

    Nkrumah writes of Congo crisis as another step in Afri-
    can revolutionary struggle. Book was written after he
    himself was deposed by coup in Ghana. His account de-
    scribes in detail series of events in Congo, always
    emphasizing role of Ghana in presence of its troops
    among UN forces and also Nkrumah's own attempts at med-
    iation. Story is told up to point of Mobutu's coup in

November 1965. Nkrumah is also particularly conscious
of interfering role of various Western powers; regards
problems of Congo as problems of all of Africa.

E. EXTERNAL RELATIONS

6. Zaire

HOSKYNS, Catherine
   The Organization of African Unity and the Congo Crisis
   1964-5 (Case Studies in African Diplomacy I, Institute
   of Public Administration; Dar es Salaam: Oxford University Press, 1969)   75 pp.
   Bibliography.

   First in series intended to help students analyze how a
   particular international dispute has arisen in Africa
   and success/failure of attempts to resolve it. Provides
   collection of documents plus introduction and chronology
   of events, intended to demonstrate role of powers outside Africa and attempts of OAU to mediate. Tries to
   present wide range of viewpoints and includes only min-
   imal editorial comment.

LEFEVER, Ernest W.
   Crisis in the Congo: a United Nations Force in action
   (Washington, D.C.: The Brookings Institution, 1965)
   215 pp.
   Bibliography.

   Analyzes, within context of international politics, the
   political, military, legal and financial aspects of UN
   forces' peacekeeping effort in Congo 1960-64; gives
   special attention to role of US support for UN operation. Uses mainly primary sources; includes appendices
   of selected documents.

LEFEVER, Ernest W.
   Uncertain Mandate: politics of the UN Congo operation
   (Baltimore, Md.: Johns Hopkins University Press, 1967)
   254 pp.
   Bibliography.

   Examines behaviour of US, Soviet Union, France, Britain,
   Belgium and Afro-Asian states in terms of their political interests and objectives in Congo operation; emphasizes political aspects, but also treats legal, administrative and military. Very thoroughly researched;
   follows other studies by Lefever.

EASTERN AFRICA

A. POLITICAL HISTORY

BRETT, E.A.
Colonialism and Underdevelopment in East Africa: the
politics of economic change 1919-1939 (London: Heinemann Educational Books, 1973) 330 pp.

This study in political economy takes an essentially
Marxist point of view which argues that 'the impact of
the relationship (between Western powers and Third
World) is profoundly ambivalent; that it tends on the
one hand to create exploitation and subjugation while on
the other it produces new forces in colonial societies
which will be capable of overthrowing external dominance
and of using positive achievements of the developed
world as a basis for the elimination of their own back-
wardness and subordination'.

DIAMOND, Stanley, and Fred G. BURKE, eds.
The Transformation of East Africa (New York: Basic
Books, 1966) 623 pp.
Bibliography.

Subtitled 'studies in political anthropology'; actually
refers to larger area of eastern Africa including Sudan,
Ethiopia, Somalia, Kenya, Uganda, Rwanda, Burundi, Tanzania, Zambia, Malawi, Mozambique. Considers various
aspects of emerging socio-political systems after independence. Emphasizes regional similarities.

HORRUT, Claude
Les Decolonisations Est-Africaines (Institut d'Etudes
Politiques de Bordeaux; Paris: Editions A. Pedone, 1971)
231 pp.
Bibliography.

Discusses respective processes of decolonization in
each of four East African countries: Kenya, Tanganyika,
Uganda, Zanzibar. Puts particular emphasis on problems
related to 'multiracialism' in context of political
evolution and conflict.

1. Ethiopia

GREENFIELD, Richard
> Ethiopia: a new political history   (London: Pall Mall Press, 1965)   515 pp.
> Bibliography.

> Analyzes history of Ethiopia's internal politics and of its particular feudal political system. Places great emphasis on attempted coup of 1960 as turning point in political development; argues that leaders of that coup sought not only to replace national leaders but to re-form whole system of government.

HESS, Robert L.
> Ethiopia: the modernization of autocracy   (Ithaca, N.Y.: Cornell University Press, 1970)   272 pp.
> Bibliography.

> Treats historical background and contemporary problems. Discusses important events of 1960s: ministerial reforms, tax innovations, 1960 coup, student riots, etc. Indicate new trends in Ethiopian political life. Concluding discussion of possible role of military is particularly interesting in light of recent events.

TREVASKIS, G.K.N.
> Eritrea: a colony in transition 1941-52   (London: Oxford University Press, 1960)   137 pp.

> History of British occupation of Eritrea; describes transition from Italian to British rule in 1941, system of government instituted by British, growth of political consciousness among Eritreans. Discusses problems related to deciding status of Eritrea after World War II and its eventual transition to autonomy in federation with Ethiopia in 1952.

2. Kenya

BENNETT, George
> Kenya - A Political History: the colonial period   (London: Oxford University Press, 1963)   190 pp.
> Bibliography.

> Political history covering period from late 19th century until eve of independence.

BUIJTENHUIJS, Robert
   Le Mouvement 'Mau-Mau': une revolte paysanne et anti-
   coloniale en Afrique-Noire   (The Hague/Paris: Mouton,
   1971)   428 pp.
   Bibliography.

   Discusses causes, characteristics and significance of
   revolt; describes Kikuyu society and its relations with
   British colonial system in Kenya.

OGOT, Bethwell A., ed.
   Politics and Nationalism in Colonial Kenya   (Nairobi:
   East African Publishing House, 1972)   275 pp.

   Proceedings of 1971 Conference of Historical Association of Kenya; mainly written by East African scholars.
   Essays on role played by different groups in nationalist
   movement in Kenya (chiefs, Mau-Mau, elders, Arabs,
   Asians, Afrikaners, trade unions, etc.).

ROSBERG, Carl G., Jr. and John NOTTINGHAM
   The Myth of Mau-Mau: nationalism in Kenya   (Hoover In-
   stitution, Stanford; New York: Praeger, 1966)   427 pp.
   Bibliography.

   Analyzes history of Kikuyu protests against colonial
   state as history of developing nationalist movement;
   argues that outbreak of violence in 1952 resulted from
   European failure to recognize need for social/political
   reform, not from failure of Kikuyu to adapt to modern
   institutional setting; argues that European concept of
   Mau-Mau was myth - maintain that Mau-Mau was integral
   part of ongoing, rationally conceived nationalist movement.

3. Malagasy Republic

PASCAL, Roger
   La Republique Malgache: pacifique independance   (Paris:
   Editions Berger-Levrault, 1965)   202 pp.
   Bibliography (largely French language).

   Discusses causes, means and effects of process of decolonization; explains failure of French colonial policy of assimilation which led the Malgaches towards
   nationalist movements; considers impact of French heritage on nation's transition to independence. Includes
   several useful appendices of documents.

SPACENSKY, Alain
  Madagascar: cinquante ans de vie politique   (Paris:
  Nouvelles Editions Latines, 1970)   526 pp.
  Bibliography.

  Very detailed study of Madagascar political system and
  its development over fifty years 1919-69; especially
  concentrates on evolution of various political parties
  and other political forces.

4. Somalia

HESS, Robert L.
  Italian Colonialism in Somalia   (Chicago: University of
  Chicago Press, 1966)   234 pp.
  Bibliography.

  Covers period 1885-1941. Discusses Italy's two experiments in government by chartered company, establishment
  of colony and its development through fascist era.
  Argues that Italian colonialism was characterized by
  lack of full commitment to responsibilities of being
  colonial power.

LEWIS, I.M.
  The Modern History of Somaliland: from nation to state
  (London: Weidenfeld & Nicloson, 1965)   234 pp.

  Political history concentrating on study of development
  from cultural to political nationalism within 'Somali
  nation'; considers effects of multiple colonization of
  single nation; describes Somaliland before partition and
  then covers period from 1860-1960. Last chapter discusses problems faced by new state.

5. Tanzania (see also Zanzibar)

LIEBENOW, J. Gus
  Colonial Rule and Political Development in Tanzania: the
  case of the Makonde (Evanston, Ill.: Northwestern University Press, 1971)   360 pp.
  Bibliography.

  How colonial heritage and other factors affected potential for political/economic development of one tribal
  group in Tanzania, particularly problem of 'capricious
  innovation' of colonial administration; Makonde region
  seen as neglected in modernizing Tanzania.

STEPHENS, Hugh W.
  The Political Transformation of Tanganyika 1920-67
  (New York: Praeger, 1968)   225 pp.
  Bibliography.

  Tries to delineate and analyze major prerequisites of
  stable nationhood and governmental effectiveness in context of Tanganyikan socio-political situation and allow-
  ing for future changes; key concept is stability and
  process involved is social mobilization; covers period
  of colonial rule, nationalist movement and independent
  state. Statistical appendix.

6. Territoire Francais des Afars et des Issas

THOMPSON, Virginia, and Richard ADLOFF
  Djibouti and the Horn of Africa   (Stanford, Calif.:
  Stanford University Press, 1968)   246 pp.
  Bibliography (mainly French language sources).

  This book is only major study in English. Part I provides historical background, description of peoples, of
  government structure and of internal/external political
  environment. Part II discusses its social development
  and describes both traditional and modern sectors of
  economy.

7. Uganda

LOW, D.A.
  Buganda in Modern History (London: Weidenfeld & Nicolson, 1971; Berkeley: University of California Press,
  1971)   265 pp.
  Bibliography.

  Examination of social and political organization of
  Buganda; 19th century conversions to Christianity; British imperial interest in Buganda; rise of nationalist
  parties before independence in 1962; and effects of independence on African states in general.

LOW, D.A.
  The Mind of Buganda: documents of the modern history of
  an African kingdom (London: Heinemann, 1971) 234 pp.

  Collection of documents relating to history of Buganda
  kingdom from 1840s to 1966; basically a study of Buganda
  as polity, especially politics as related to cultural
  destiny.

8. Zanzibar

AYANY, Samuel G.
> A History of Zanzibar: a study in constitutional development 1934-1964 (Nairobi: East Africa Literature Bureau, 1970)   208 pp.
> Bibliography.

After providing introduction to broader environment in Zanzibar and its history, discusses political/constitutional development with historical approach. Emphasizes period leading to independence in 1963, but also adds epilogue to cover revolution which overthrew Arab oligarchy and which led up to union with Tanganyika.

B. POLITICAL SYSTEMS, GOVERNMENT

1. Ethiopia

CLAPHAM, Christopher
> Haile Selassie's Government (London: Longmans, Green & Co. Ltd., 1969)   218 pp.
> Bibliography.

Describes and analyzes Ethiopia's central government and its development between liberation from Italian occupation in 1941 and end of 1967. In particular, studies constitutional framework, role of emperor, various political groupings, high officials, imperial secretariat, central institutions, parliament, etc. Includes biographical appendix plus useful tables related to chronology, genealogy, and structure of government.

GILKES, Patrick
> The Dying Lion: feudalism and modernization in Ethiopia (London: Julian Friedmann, 1975)   307 pp.
> Bibliography.

Book attempts to analyze some of causes of 1974 crisis and to identify power groupings which have relevance in Ethiopian politics. Includes analysis of class structures, both major traditional classes and those that have emerged since World War II. Describes national movements and opposition in Amhara, Tigre, Eritrea, Oromo and Somali groups as well as contradictions existing within ruling class.

LECLERCQ, Claude
    L'Empire d'Ethipie (Encyclopedie Politique et Consti-
tutionnelle, Institut International d'Administration
Publique; Paris: Editions Berger-Levrault, 1969) 79 pp.
Bibliography.

    Outlines historical context, demographic, cultural and
    social factors, economy/finances, judicial and political
    factors. Discusses Ethiopian policies: internal absol-
    ute monarchy and external ordered progress. Appendices
    include text of 1955 Constitution and 1966 Imperial
    order delimiting powers of ministers.

MARKAKIS, John
    Ethiopia: anatomy of a traditional polity (Oxford:
Clarendon Press, 1974) 409 pp.
Bibliography.

    Analyzes class structures and ethnic groupings which
    play role in polity; examines patterns of change re-
    sulting from education, urbanization and emerging mid-
    dle class. Discusses relationship between emerging
    social structure and distribution and uses of power;
    attempts to evaluate efficiency of utilization of power
    in political system in pursuit of certain goods.

PERHAM, Margery
    The Government of Ethiopia (London: Faber & Faber,
1969) Second edition. 531 pp.
Bibliography.

    First edition was published in 1948 and was standard
    work on this subject. Introduction to 1969 edition is
    historical survey of 1946-68, especially foreign rela-
    tions and internal affairs. Appendix A, by C. Clapham,
    discusses development of central government in 1946-68.
    Other appendices include Constitution of 1955, treaties,
    chronology of events since 1941. Main text on govern-
    ment of Ethiopia covers monarchy, central institutions,
    church, law/justice, army, public finance, slavery,
    health/education, provincial governments, and short
    discussion of Anglo-Ethiopian relations. Still consid-
    ered to be most authoritative work on Ethiopian politics.

SCHWAB, Peter
    Decision-making in Ethiopia: a study of the political
process (London: C. Hurst & Co., 1972) 201 pp.
Bibliography.

    Case study focusing on Agricultural Income Tax Bill of

1966-67, studies political process and analyzes interaction between forces of modernization and tradition in
Ethiopia. Studies not only passage of bill in parliament, but implementation process as well.

2. Kenya

ARNOLD, Guy
Kenyatta and the Politics of Kenya   (London: J.M. Dent
& Sons, Ltd., 1974)   226 pp.
Bibliography.

Not biography of Kenyatta; rather, examines Kenyatta's
influence on Kenya's political development. Traces
evolution of Kenya from 1890s, at time when Kenyatta
was born; discusses Kenyatta's consolidation of unity
in Kenya, but perhaps is not critical enough until final
pages. Leaves many questions about what will come after
Kenyatta.

GERTZEL, Cherry
The Politics of Independent Kenya 1963-68 (Nairobi:
East African Publishing House, 1970; London: Heinemann,
1970)   180 pp.

Describes most significant events in first five years
of Kenyan independence in this series of essays. Primarily concerned with political realignments which resulted from resignation of Vice-President Oginga Odinga
in April 1966 and his formation of Kenya People's Union
Party.

GERTZEL, Cherry, Maure GOLDSCHMIDT, and Donald ROTHCHILD, eds.
Government and Politics in Kenya: a nation-building text
(Nairobi: East African Publishing House, 1969)   611 pp.

Comprehensive study, ideal for students in analysis of
political systems. Parts II to X cover problems of
nation-building: race, tribe, religion, geographical
imbalances, income class, occupation, employment, corruption; political parties and interest groups; parliamentary system; central administration; local administration; functions of government.

HORRUT, Claude
La Republique du Kenya (Encyclopedie Politique et Con-
stitutionnelle, Institut International d'Administration
Publique; Paris: Editions Berger-Levrault, 1972) 77 pp.
Bibliography.

Provides resume of Kenyan socio-political context and
its political/constitutional evolution up to 1972.
Includes full text of Kenyan constitution.

HYDEN, Goran, Robert JACKSON, and John OKUMU, eds.
Development Administration: the Kenyan experience
(Nairobi: Oxford University Press, 1970) 366 pp.
Bibliography.

Considers relation between public administration and development problems in Kenya; studies what sort of organization is adapted to problems of change, i.e.,
deals with impact of social, political, economic forces
upon government administration, with some internal operations of civil service, and ability of public administrators and their organizations to affect, alter and
reshape external environments which surround them.

LEYS, Colin
Underdevelopment in Kenya: the political economy of
neo-colonialism 1964-1971 (London: Heinemann, 1975)
284 pp.

Uses theoretical framework from work of 'underdevelopment' and 'dependency' theorists as his perspective --
an entirely new approach to study of Kenya. Discusses
transition from colonial economy to neo-colonialism
(post-independence) and African capitalism; analyzes
its consequences in terms of social class structure and
finally, political manifestations/change.

WERLIN, Herbert H.
Governing an African City: a study of Nairobi (New
York: Africana Publishing Co., 1974) 308 pp.

Based on author's theoretical framework which he calls
'elasticity of control', i.e., when political control
is reponsive to variations of need; discusses relationship between politicians and administrators, between
between governmental units in single-party system;
problems of both centralization and decentralization in
ldc's, etc.

3. Malagasy Republic

CADOUX, Charles
La Republique Malgache (encyclopedie Politique et Con-
stitutionnelle, Institut d'Administration Publique;
Paris: Editions Berger-Levrault, 1969) 123 pp.
Bibliography.

Follows general plan of series, with discussion of contemporary society, political forces and basic principles
underlying present political system. Includes text of
of constitution.

THOMPSON, Virginia and Richard ADLOFF
The Malagasy Republic: Madagascar Today (Stanford, Cal-
if.: Stanford University Press, 1965)   504 pp.
Bibliography.

General survey of history, politics, social, economic
aspects. Especially interesting account of Malagasy
national character and its effect on post-independence
political development.

4. Somalia

CONTINI, Paolo
The Somali Republic: an experiment in legal integration
(London: Frank Cass & Co., Ltd., 1969)   92 pp.
Bibliography.

Written by chairman of Consultative Commission for Integration (to assist Somali government in bringing a-
bout legislative unification of British Somaliland and
Italian Somalia). Surveys steps leading to independence
and formation of Somali Republic; describes progress
made in process of legislative integration; also attempts
to illustrate interaction among different legal systems
coexisting in country and their respective impact on
constitution, laws and judicial decisions.

LEWIS, I.M.
A Pastoral Democracy: a study of pastoralism and poli-
tics among the Northern Somali of the Horn of Africa
(International African Institute; London: Oxford Univ-
ersity Press, 1961)   320 pp.
Bibliography.

Comprehensive study of pastoral habits and political
institutions of Northern Somali (political anthropology
approach). Discusses lineage structure as general
principle of political association and form of social
contract as organizing political relations; emphasizes
importance of force as ultimate arbiter in political
relations. Also discusses relation between traditional
political structures and modern governmental administration.

5. Tanzania (see also Zanzibar)

CLIFFE, Lionel and John S. SAUL, eds.
Socialism in Tanzania, Volume One: Politics (Nairobi:
East African Publishing House, 1972) 346 pp.

Thirty-seven essays, articles and papers covering economic and political background of Tanzania and Zanzibar.
Focuses on contemporary social, economic and idelogical
setting in which socialist politics have emerged; detailed discussion of government and party institutions.

DRYDEN, Stanley
Local Administration in Tanzania (Nairobi: East African
Publishing House, 1968) 178 pp.
Bibliography.

Analyzes foundation structures which date from colonial
period and how they have been modified, added onto, etc.
to accommodate needs of new Tanzanian state; includes
particular reference to one-party state and structures
that have been created for it in order to transform
political system.

INGLE, Clyde R.
From Village to State in Tanzania: the politics of rural
development (Ithaca, N.Y.: Cornell University Press,
1972) 279 pp.
Bibliography.

Analyzes linkages between selected village political
systems and national system in two districts of Tanzania
(Tanga and Handeni) in order to show how these intermed-
iate political systems are used to bring national goals
into rural village communities.

MAGUIRE, G. Andrew
Toward 'Uhuru' in Tanzania: the politics of participation
(London: Cambridge University Press, 1969) 403 pp.
Bibliography.

Micropolitical historical study of Sukumaland, beginning
with emergence of indigenous politics; studied in context of Tanzania's unique political context: in that its
political leadership under one regime since independence
continues to attempt to give effect to mix of traditional and modern, socialist and democratic principles;
argues that they have succeeded partially in important
ways.

SAMOFF, Joel
   Tanzania: local politics and the structure of power
   (Madison: University of Wisconsin Press, 1974)   286 pp.
   Bibliography.

   Study of local politics in Moshi, Tanzania, largely
   concerned with relationship of structures of local power to socio-political change;   explores implementation
   of development objectives in local context and examines
   role of local politics in providing base for democratic
   participation.   Concentrates on TANU.

TORDOFF, W.
   Government and Politics in Tanzania   (Nairobi: East African Publishing House, 1967)   257 pp.

   Collection of essays covering period from September
   1960 to July 1966.   Theme is relationship between organs
   of government and single party.

URFER, Sylvain
   La Republique Unie de Tanzanie   (Encyclopedie Politique
   et Constitutionnelle, Institut International d'Administration Publique; Paris: Editions Berger-Levrault,
   1973)   91 pp.
   Bibliography.

   Provides concise description of Tanzanian society and
   of political/constitutional evolution, including political forces before and after independence.   Includes
   texts of several important documents.

7. Uganda

APTER, David E.
   The Political Kingdom in Uganda: a study in bureaucra-
   tic nationalism   (Princeton, N.J.: Princeton University
   Press, 1967)   Second edition.   498 pp.

   Study in political development of Buganda as a modernizing autocracy; studies ambiguities of Buganda politics
   especially how new state of Uganda was forced to choose
   between increasing ethnic strife or change of modernizing autocracy into modern state with representative
   government.   Apter traces development up to early efforts to create modern representative government after
   expulsion of Kabaka of Buganda.

BURKE, Fred G.
  Local Government and Politics in Uganda   (New York: Syr-
  acuse University Press, 1964)   274 pp.
  Bibliography.

  Study focuses on districts of Bunyoro-Kitara, Teso and
  Bukedi; concerned with relation of evolution of local
  political systems to development of Ugandan nation.
  Three districts chosen provide comparison of different
  types of traditional systems and how they have been
  adapted to modern political life.

GERTZEL, Cherry
  Party and Locality in Northern Uganda, 1945-1962
  (Institute of Commonwealth Studies, University of London,
  Commonwealth Papers 16; The Athlone Press, 1974) 100 pp.
  Bibliography.

  Study of African nationalism via political developments
  (growth of political parties) in Acholi and Lango districts of Uganda. An example of trend towards micropoli-
  tics.

GUKIINA, Peter M.
  Uganda: a case study in African political development
  (Notre Dame, Ind.: Notre Dame University Press, 1972)
  190 pp.
  Bibliography.

  Attempts to analyze main political and cultural forces
  in Uganda which brought about political system different
  from that 'desired and hoped for by the overwhelming
  majority of Ugandans'. Examines presence or absence of
  national consensus at time of independence and examines
  in detail successes and failures of Obote's efforts to
  create national political system. Author's conclusions
  concerning General Amin seem somewhat naive in light of
  current events.

8. Zanzibar

LOFCHIE, Michael F.
  Zanzibar: background to revolution   (Princeton, N.J.:
  Princeton University Press, 1965)   316 pp.
  Bibliography.

  This analysis of Zanzibar's political system is based
  largely on political struggle between Arab minority and
  African majority; discusses development of respective
  political parties, fact that race tended to coincide

with economic class, and British role in perpetuating
these racial imbalances; provides clear analysis of conditions which finally brought about coup by African party. Analysis ends at time of merger with Tanganyika.

MIDDLETON, John and Jane CAMPBELL
Zanzibar: its society and its politics (Institute of
Race Relations; London: Oxford University Press, 1965)
71 pp.
Bibliography.

Provides description of historical socio-political environment which led to revolution of 1964, but was written
too early to include analysis of revolution itself.
Especially useful is chapter on parties and politics,
including elections of 1957, 1961, 1963.

C. POLITICAL PARTIES, INTEREST GROUPS AND IDEOLOGIES

GHAI, Dharam P. and Yash P. GHAI, eds.
Portrait of a Minority: Asians in East Africa (Nairobi:
Oxford University Press, 1970) Revised edition. 227 pp.

Discusses social, political, economic and educational
aspects of life of Asian immigrant minority in East Africa; of particular interest as study of minority in
plural society. Final chapter discusses uncertainties
in future prospects: says that it is up to Asians (who
are African citizens and choose to stay) to work out
their future role in rapidly changing African societies.

GULLIVER, P.H., ed.
Tradition and Transition in East Africa: studies of the
tribal element in the modern era (London: Routledge &
Kegan Paul, 1969)   378 pp.
Bibliography.

Case studies of tribes rather than tribalism. Good introduction by Gulliver in which he says that tribalism
is variant of particularism.

MAZRUI, Ali A.
Cultural Engineering and Nation-Building in East Africa
(Evanston, Ill.: Northwestern University Press, 1972)
301 pp.

Theoretical work on nature of society in East Africa;
attempts to identify major elements of 'purposeful cultural manipulation' in relation to social policy; deals
with problem of 'identity' through communication in

language and literature; and deals with phenomenon of
classes in transition and its implications for political
systems.

MEISTER, Albert
East Africa: the past in chains, the future in pawn
(New York: Walker & Co., 1968) 282 pp.

Originally published in French as 'L'Afrique Peut-Elle
Partir' (Paris: Editions du Seuil, 1966). Analyzes some
of characteristics of traditional society and discusses
problems involved in clash between modern and traditional societies; shows how insufficient destruction of traditional framework is jeopardizing development; emphasizes role of myths and ideologies.

PREWITT, Kenneth, ed.
Education and Political Values: an East African case
study (Nairobi: East African Publishing House, 1971)
249 pp.

Series of essays stressing various aspects of political
socialization through education, student politics in
higher education; demonstrates links between educational
practices of East African countries and political beliefs
of citizens.

RICHARDS, Audrey J.
The Multicultural States of East Africa (Montreal:
McGill-Queen's University Press, 1969) 123 pp.
Bibliography.

From series of lectures delivered in 1966. Studies ethnic diversity in new East African states, effects of
independence on ethnic rivalries (Uganda case study),
role of ethnic diversity in rural development programmes
and finally, considers integrating forces.

1. Ethiopia

LEVINE, Donald N.
Wax and Gold: tradition and innovation in Ethiopian cul-
ture (Chicago: University of Chicago Press, 1965)315 pp.
Bibliography.

Treats relation between tradition and modernity as it
appears in variety of social and cultural phenomena:
bases of cultural identity among Amhara; background to
ethnic regionalism; peasants; contrasting socialization
of youth through education; elite structures.

2. Kenya

BENNETT, George and Carl G. ROSBERG
The Kenyatta Election, Kenya 1960-61 (Institute of Commonwealth Studies, Oxford; London: Oxford University Press) 230 pp.

Election study of first Kenyan election which led to major shift in power from colonialists to local communities, with Africans holding majority in Legislative Council -- first major step towards independent state. Studies background and campaigns, electoral machinery.

BIENEN, Henry
Kenya: the politics of participation and control
Princeton, N.J.: Princeton University Press, 1974)
215 pp.
Bibliography (16 pp.).

Concerned with African politics in Kenya (leaves out non-African interest groups); examines Civil Service and KANU, both as vehicles for channeling demands and for controlling political behaviour; leads to discussion of ethnic, class and factional divisions in Kenyan politics. Makes little reference to economic interest groups.

ROTHCHILD, Donald
Racial Bargaining in Independent Kenya: a study of minorities and decolonization (Institute of Race Relations, London; London: Oxford University Press, 1973) 476 pp.

Change from European-dominated society towards African one is analyzed in terms of model of shifting bargaining relationships among three main racial communities. Includes problems such as Africanization programmes and citizenship.

SANDBROOK, Richard
Proletarians and African Capitalism: the Kenyan case 1960-72 (Perspectives on Development Series No. 4; London: Cambridge University Press, 1975) 222 pp.

Studies role of unionized workers in Kenya within larger analysis of Kenyan political economy. Includes both union-government relations and internal union politics; discusses motivations and political actions of workers in context of Kenya's capitalist economic strategy.

SINGH, Makhan
    History of Kenya's Trade Union Movement to 1952 (Nairobi:
    East African Publishing House, 1969)   332 pp.

    Author is and was activist in labour movement and nation-
    alist movement. Describes evolution of trade unions in
    context of broader struggle for independence; includes
    extensive documentation plus personal knowledge of auth-
    or.

5. Tanzania

BIENEN, Henry
    Tanzania: party transformation and economic development
    (Princeton, N.J.: Princeton University Press, 1970)
    506 pp.
    Bibliography.

    Critical study of an African one-party state and its
    role in bringing about economic and social change; ana-
    lyzes organization, recruitment and ideology and relation
    between them of TANU, especially during 1960's; includes
    discussion of Arusha Declaration.

CLIFFE, Lionel, ed.
    One-Party Democracy: the 1965 Tanzania general elections
    (Nairobi: East African Publishing House, 1967)   470 pp.
    Bibliography.

    Analysis of election which was Tanzania's first experi-
    ment in 'single party democracy', to choose those indi-
    viduals preferred as national representatives by Tangan-
    yika African National Union and by electorate. Book
    makes no judgments about whether or not this is really
    'democracy', but rather analyzes circumstances of elec-
    tion and political processes surrounding it; contains
    much detail including maps of voting districts, actual
    voting results, etc.

FRIEDLAND, William H.
    'Vuta Kamba': the development of trade unions in Tangan-
    yika (Stanford, Calif.: Hoover Institution Press, 1969)
    280 pp.
    Bibliography.

    Studies factors involved when an institutional form is
    developed in one cultural context and then introduced
    into a different one, i.e., what sort of changes were
    introduced into trade unions as social institution;

uses concept of 'transfer model' to demonstrate which
institutional elements were transformed and how.

HOPKINS, Raymond F.
Political Roles in a New State: Tanzania's first decade
(New Haven: Yale University Press, 1971) 293 pp.

Two main objectives are to explore character of national
politics in Tanzania from perspective of members of
political elite and to apply theories developed in analysis of roles to empirical data collected from sample
of Tanzanian elite. Focuses on institutionalization of
role norms, i.e., the rules of new political system.

HYDEN, Goran
TANU Yajenga Nchi: political development in rural Tan-
zania (Lund Political Studies 8; Lund, Sweden: UNISKOL,
Bokforlaget Universitet och Skola, 1968) 282 pp.
Bibliography.

Studies relations between rural inhabitants of Buhaya
(part of Tanzania) and central political system; focuses on role of TANU in studying problems of identity,
legitimacy, penetration, allocation and participation;
considered in terms of rural attitudes to development.
Book includes summary written in Kiswahili.

PROCTOR, J.H., ed.
The Cell System of the Tanganyika African National Union
(University of Dar es Salaam, Studies in Political Science no. 1; Dar es Salaam: Tanzania Publishing House,
1971) 66 pp.

Six studies based on direct observation of cell system
at work; compare operation in various parts of Tanzania
and reveal great variety in organization and performance of cells, not only as between rural and urban settings but also from one rural area to another.

URFER, Sylvain
Ujamaa: espoir du socialisme africain en Tanzanie
(Collection Tiers Monde et Developpement; Paris: Aubier
Montaigne, 1971) 239 pp.
Bibliography.

Provides historical/ideological analysis of Tanzanian
socialism; emphasis on socialism as expounded by Julius
Nyerere. Includes documents such as Tanganyika-Zanzibar
Treaty, Arusha Declaration.

7. Uganda

FALLERS, Lloyd A., ed.
The King's Men: leadership and status in Buganda on the eve of independence (London: Oxford University Press, 1964) 414 pp.
Bibliography.

Political anthropology approach based on study of social stratification, social mobility, leadership and authority -- in each case, authors have contrasted traditional and modern Buganda; studies are intended to help understanding of substructure of contemporary Buganda politics, though analyses relate to pre-independence period.

LEYS, Colin
Politicians and Policies: an essay on politics in Acholi, Uganda 1962-65 (Nairobi: East African Publishing House, 1967; reprinted 1972) 107 pp.

Studies political concerns of district elite in Acholi; therefore, focuses on content of public policy as well as on structure and function.

SCOTT, Roger
The Development of Trade Unions in Uganda (Nairobi: East African Publishing House, 1966) 200 pp.
Bibliography.

Describes and analyzes development of trade unions in context of Ugandan plural society and of nationalist movement.

WELBOURN, F.B.
Religion and Politics in Uganda, 1952-62 (Nairobi: East African Publishing House, 1965) 78 pp.

Studies search for new ethnic identity to contain disintegrating effects on Buganda of Muslim and Christian missions, in context of rise to power of Uganda People's Congress (UPC) under Dr. Milton Obote.

D. BIOGRAPHIES, MEMOIRS, SPEECHES, WRITINGS BY POLITICAL LEADERS

BENNETT, Norman R., ed.
Leadership in Eastern Africa: six political biographies (Boston: Boston University Press, 1968)

Study of six African leaders in East and Central Africa and their relations with Europeans in 19th-20th centuries.

1. Ethiopia

MOSLEY, Leonard
> Haile Selassie: the conquering lion   (London: Weidenfeld &Nicolson, 1964)   306 pp.
> Bibliography.

Biography of Haile Selassie. Besides providing interesting account of personal development of Haile Selassie, provides insights into processes of government in Ethiopia and autocratic power of royal family, but is a bit sensationalistic.

2. Kenya

KAGGIA, Bildad
> Roots of Freedom 1921-63   (Nairobi: East African Publishing House, 1975)   202 pp.

Autobiography of prominent Kenyan nationalist and politician. Treats some of more controversial aspects of Kenyan political history including morality of oathing and stress on unity in face of external threat; historical significance of Mau-Mau struggle and origins of Kenyatta's leadership; special position of ex-detainees; conflict between wishes of masses and party machine.

KENYATTA, Jomo
> Suffering Without Bitterness: the founding of the Kenya nation (Nairobi: East African Publishing House, 1968) 348 pp.

Kenyatta discusses, from his own point of view, facts and background of events which preceded his arrest and imprisonment, and subsequent patterns which led to his release and assumption of leadership in Kenya government. Appendix is collection of speeches dating from Kenya independence in 1963 to celebration of Kenyatta Day in 1967.

KINDY, Hyder
> Life and Politics in Mombasa   (Nairobi: East African Publishing House, 1972)   236 pp.

Autobiography of local political leader gives inside view of local politics in crucial area of Kenya. His description of Swahili life in Mombasa is particularly interesting.

LUBEMBE, Clement K.
   The Inside of the Labour Movement in Kenya   (Nairobi:
   Equatorial Publishers, 1968)   240 pp.
   Bibliography.

   Written by Kenyan leader of trade unions. Discusses
   evolution of trade unions in Kenya and their role in
   context of political development. Book is obviously
   pro-trade union and pro-wage labour. Includes several
   relevant documents.

MBOYA, Tom
   The Challenge of Nationhood   (London: Andre Deutsch,
   1970)   278 pp.

   Collection of speeches and writings of former minister
   in Kenya government; covers topics related to Kenya's
   development, Pan-Africanism, Africa's role in world.

MBOYA, Tom
   Freedom and After   (London: Andre Deutsch, 1963) 272 pp.

   Autobiography, describes Mboya's life until just before
   Kenyan independence. Is therefore story of one man's
   participation in successful nationalist movement.

MURRAY-BROWN, Jeremy
   Kenyatta   (London: George Allen & Unwin, 1972)   381 pp.

   Not an 'authorized' biography, but very well researched
   critical biography. Much attention paid to Kenyatta's
   Kikuyu background and his early contact with whites.
   Fits Kenyatta's life into political/economic development
   of Kenya.

ODINGA, Oginga
   Not Yet Uhuru: an autobiography of Oginga Odinga   (London: Heinemann, 1967)   323 pp.

   Autobiography of Kenyan nationalist who, since independence, had broken with ruling party. Therefore, provides critical analsis of path of development taken in
   Kenya since independence, including period when author
   himself was minister of home affairs in government.

4. Somalia

TOUVAL, Saadia
   Somali Nationalism: international politics and the
   drive for unity in the Horn of Africa   (Cambridge, Mass.:
   Harvard University Press, 1963)   214 pp.

Studies Somali claims for national self-determination
and unification, and their effect on regional and international politics. Clear example of consequences of
colonialist partitioning of Africa in which states did
not correspond to nations.

5. Tanzania

ILIFFE, John, ed.
Modern Tanzanians: a volume of biographies (Nairobi:
East African Publishing House, 1973)   258 pp.

Biographies written by students of Dar es Salaam University History Department. Includes lives of thirteen men,
all of whom have been 'innovators' in Tanzania, although
they may be differentiated according to their scale of
action and degree of change which they tried to introduce.

NYERERE, Julius K.
Freedom and Unity - Uhuru na Umoja (London: Oxford
University Press, 1967)   366 pp.

Selection of writings and speeches 1952-65 by current
president of Tanzania. First of three volumes: each
volume contains useful introduction; collection of
speeches provides good insights into nature of TANU government and of Tanzanian brand of socialism; also provides greater understanding of Nyerere as individual.

NYERERE, Julius K.
Freedom and Socialism - Uhuru na Ujamaa (London: Oxford
University Press, 1968)   422 pp.

Selection of writings and speeches from 1965-67: statements not of what now exists in Tanzania, but of what is
being aimed at.

NYERERE, Julius K.
Freedom and Development - Uhuru na Maendeleo (London:
Oxford University Press, 1973)   400 pp.

Selection of writings and speeches from 1968-73.

NYERERE, Julius K.
Ujamaa: essays on socialism (London: Oxford University
Press, 1968)   186 pp.

Booklet intended to elaborate further on Arusha Declaration policy implications and on relation between socialist philosophy and other doctrines of life and society.
Meant to lead to understanding of moral principles,
aspirations, methods of Tanzanian development.

7. Uganda

IBINGIRA, G.S.K.
> The Forging of an African Nation: the political and
> constitutional evolution of Uganda from colonial rule to
> independence 1894-1962 (New York: Viking Press, 1973)
> 332 pp.
> Bibliography.

Author was himself a founder member of UPC and has been
continuously active in Ugandan politics. Book is very
much a personal account of evolution of Ugandan nation;
author attempts to convey effect of various political
and cultural pressures associated with Uganda's constitution-making processes.

8. Zanzibar

OKELLO, John
> Revolution in Zanzibar (Nairobi: East African Publish-
> ing House, 1967)   222 pp.

Autobiography of man who led revolution against Sultan
of Zanzibar's government in January 1964; revolution
was successful but Okello was thrown out. Book is his
account of how revolution took place and his role in it.

E. EXTERNAL RELATIONS

DOIMI DI DELUPIS, Ingrid
> The East African Community and Common Market (London:
> Longmans, 1970)   185 pp.
> Bibliography.

Emphasizes history, economic aspects and law involved,
but is of interest to students of politics as well.
Gives detailed information on institutional structure of
East African Community, its powers, its common services
and its relations with rest of world (especially EEC).

HUGHES, A.J.
> East Africa: the search for unity (Harmondsworth, Mid-
> dlesex: Penguin, 1963)   271 pp.

Considers development of each of four East African states
(Tanganyika, Kenya, Uganda, Zanzibar). Describes diffi-
culties in search for federation and in securing simul-
taneous independence. As study was written in 1963,
only considers idea of original unity attempts, but
does not follow up evolution of East African Federation.

LEYS,Colin and Peter ROBSON, eds.
   Federation in East Africa: opportunities and problems
   (Nairobi: Oxford University Press, 1965)   244 pp.
   Bibliography.

   Papers discuss political and economic aspects of possible federation: where economic common market already
   existed but political federation required greater impe-
   tus of common interest, etc. Authors are, on the whole,
   favourable towards idea of federation.

NYE, Joseph S., Jr.
   Pan-Africanism and East African Integration   (Cambridge,
   Mass.: Harvard University Press, 1966)   307 pp.
   Bibliography.

   Concerned with Pan-Africanism as ideology and its effects
   in real terms on political integration attempts; in
   particular, studies failure to create East African Federation in 1963. Based on 115 formal interviews with
   politicians.

ROTHCHILD, Donald, ed.
   Politics of Integration: an East African documentary
   (Nairobi: East African Publishing House, 1968)   343 pp.
   Bibliography.

   Collection of documents concerned with major political
   and economic experiments in cooperation within East
   Africa from 1920 until 1967 treaty.

4. Somalia

DRYSDALE, John
   The Somali Dispute   (London: Pall Mall Press, 1964)
   183 pp.

   Provides historical background to demarcation of Somali
   boundaries by various colonial powers and discusses
   problems related to Somali nationalism.

5. Tanzania

YU, George T.
   China and Tanzania: a study in cooperative interaction
   (Centre for Chinese Studies, No. 5, University of Cal-
   ifornia, Berkeley, 1970)   100 pp.

   Study intended to show one example of China's foreign
   policy. Hypothesis is that China and Tanzania have
   evolved 'partial informal alliance'.

FORMER PORTUGUESE AFRICA

A. POLITICAL HISTORY

CHILCOTE, Ronald H.
  Portuguese Africa   (Englewood Cliffs, N.J.: Prentice-
  Hall, 1967)   149 pp.
  Bibliography.

  First three chapters introduce Portuguese colonial system: policy and institutional forces, Portuguese and
  African nationalism; followed by chapter each on Angola,
  Mozambique and Portuguese Guinea, concentrating on political, economic, social and cultural trends in each.

DUFFY, James
  Portugal in Africa   (Harmondsworth, Middlesex: Penguin
  African Library, Penguin Books, 1962)   240 pp.
  Bibliography.

  Brief political history of Portuguese presence in Africa,
  with emphasis on colonies of Angola and Mozambique.

EHNMARK, Anders, and Per WASTBERG
  Angola and Mozambique: the case against Portugal   (London: Pall Mall Press, 1963)   176 pp.

  Two entirely separate essays; descriptions and indict-
  ments of Portugal's colonial policy in these two colonies; both emphasize economic and cultural exploitation.

1. Angola

CHILCOTE, Ronald H.
  Protest and Resistance in Angola and Brazil: comparative
  studies   (Berkeley/Los Angeles: University of California
  Press, 1972)   317 pp.

  Angolan essays emphasize means used by Angolans to avoid
  being integrated into Portuguese-dominated society;
  those on Brazil focus more on problems of political,
  economic and social integration and on power struggles
  within both local and national contexts (relates to
  Northeast region of Brazil); concludes with classifica-
  tion of pre-nationalist movements in Brazil and Portuguese Africa in order to reveal wide range of examples
  of protest and resistance.

MARCUM, John
 The Angolan Revolution, Volume I: the anatomy of an ex-
 plosion 1950-62 (Cambridge, Mass.: MIT Press, 1969)
 380 pp.

Part I discusses rise of Angolan nationalism before revolution (1950-60) in form of political groupings based
on precolonial ethnic and regional origins. Part II
describes 1961 as year of rebellion; deals with various
Angolan responses to northern rebellion and with struggle
for revolutionary leadership between various nationalist
groups; also considers world responses to rebellion.
Part III describes transition to revolution, guerilla
war and government in exile; studies American, Portuguese and colonial response to revolution and political
manoeuvering within revolutionary movements. Five com-
plementary appendices.

B. POLITICAL SYSTEMS, GOVERNMENT

ABSHIRE, David B., and A. SAMUELS, eds.
 Portuguese Africa: a handbook (London: Pall Mall Press,
 1969) 480 pp.

Interdisciplinary study; background material, government
and society, economy, political and internal issues;
considerable amount of useful data. Emphasizes Portuguese colonial policies rather than nationalist movements.

1. Angola

WHEELER, Douglas L., and Rene PELISSIER
 Angola (London: Pall Mall Press, 1971)   296 pp.
 Bibliography.

Wheeler's part one provides history of Portuguese colonialism and discussion of origins of Angolan nationalism;
in particular, studies 1926-61, period of classic colonial rule, free of anti-colonial pressures but in which
can be found origins of anti-colonial insurgency which
began in 1961. Pelissier's part two describes political
cooperation before 1961, armed revolt of 1961 and political aftermath of revolt until 1970; concludes with discussion of socio-economic situation in Angola. Wheeler
contributes brief chapter as part three concerned with
international politics. Book is most up-to-date survey
of Angola, concentrating on origins of political consciousness and detailed account of Angolan movements.

2. Guinea-Bissau

RUDEBECK, Lars
  Guinea-Bissau: a study of political mobilization (Upp-
  sala, Sweden: The Scandinavian Institute of African
  Studies, 1974)   277 pp.
  Bibliography.

  Provides historical background to Portuguese colonial
  systems and formation of PAIGC; discusses ideology and
  goals of PAIGC; main body of book studies emerging social order in Guinea-Bissau including political, administrative, military and judicial organization, election
  campaign and elections of 1972, economic, social and
  cultural organization. Particularly useful for its description of new society being constructed by PAIGC even
  while armed struggle continued. Concludes with theoretical remarks concerning political mobilization.

C. POLITICAL PARTIES, INTEREST GROUPS AND IDEOLOGIES

CHILCOTE, Ronald H.
  Emerging Nationalism in Portuguese Africa: documents
  (Stanford, Calif.: Hoover Institution Press, 1972)

  Major documentary collection describing origin, organization, leadership and ideology of nationalist groups
  in Portuguese Africa; translations of 179 documents;
  numerous tables with charts showing origin and growth of
  parties.

1. Angola

DAVIDSON, Basil
  In the Eye of the Storm: Angola's people (London: Long-
  mans, 1972)   355 pp.
  Bibliography.

  Journalist's analysis of Angolan situation based on personal experience in guerilla-held areas; favourable to
  guerillas; includes historical setting, recent events,
  discussion of aims/objectives relevant to Angola's
  people.

OKUMA, Thomas
  Angola in Ferment: the background and prospects of Angolan nationalism (Boston: Beacon Press, 1962)   137 pp.

  Foreward by Rupert Emerson. Author was missionary in
  Angola for some time. Examines forces which gave birth
  to African nationalist movements in Angola; views clash

in Angola as between two nationalisms: Portuguese and
African; examines disruptive forces of West, attacks on
Portugal in United Nations by Afro-Asian groups, alliance
of USA with Portugal. Appendices provide documents regarding religious societies and other movements.

2. Guinea-Bissau

CHALIAN, Gerard
> Armed Struggle in Africa with the Guerillas in Portu-
> guese Guinea   (New York: Monthly Review Press, 1969)
> 142 pp.
> Bibliography.

> Based on author's travels in 1966 with Amilcar Cabral
> and other PAIGC leaders through liberated territory in
> Guinea; takes pro-guerilla standpoint; emphasizes struc-
> ture of resistance movement, its political strategies,
> role played by leaders, cadres, fighters, peasants at all
> levels of struggle. Appendices relate to Portuguese
> psychological warfare and foreign interests.

DAVIDSON, Basil
> The Liberation of Guine: aspects of an African revolution
> (Harmondsworth, Middlesex: Penguin African Library, Pen-
> guin Books, 1969)
> Bibliography.

> Study of guerilla warfare in African context: PAIGC
> movement against Portuguese in Guinea-Bissau; much infor-
> mation taken from first-hand sources; introduction by
> Amilcar Cabral, leader of PAIGC.

D. BIOGRAPHIES, MEMOIRS, SPEECHES, WRITINGS
BY POLITICAL LEADERS

3. Mozambique

MONDLANE, Eduardo
> The Struggle for Mozambique   (Harmondsworth, Middlesex:
> Penguin African Library, Penguin Books, 1969) 222 pp.

> Author was president of FRELIMO until his assassination
> in 1969. Attempts to show real effects of Portuguese
> colonization upon African; traces origins of war in
> social structure, education and economic exploitation;
> describes development of resistance movement, its goals
> and its impact on African society in Mozambique.

E. EXTERNAL RELATIONS

MINTER, William
    Portuguese Africa and the West   (Harmondsworth, Middle-
    sex: Penguin African Library, Penguin Books, 1972)
    176 pp.
    Bibliography.

    Discusses American policy with regard to Portugal and
    its African colonies; indicts West (USA and others) for
    support of colonialism - both military, political and
    economic.

SOUTHERN AFRICA

A. POLITICAL HISTORY

STEVENS, Richard P.
Lesotho, Botswana and Swaziland: the former High Commis-
sion Territories in Southern Africa (London: Pall Mall
Press, 1967) 294 pp.
Bibliography.

Comparative political history; considers each of three
territories separately, integrating discussion in introduction and conclusion. Emphasizes British administration, processes leading to independence and relations
with South Africa.

1. Botswana

SILLERY, Anthony
Botswana: a short political history (London: Methuen &
Co., Ltd., 1974) 219 pp.
Bibliography.

Begins with arrival of missionaries in early 19th century; discusses changing political status of Bechuanaland, political relations with Britain and local politics
up to independence in 1966. Emphasizes character of
Tswana people.

3. Malawi

FRANKLIN, Harry
Unholy Wedlock: the failure of the Central African Federation (London: George Allen & Unwin, 1963) 239 pp.

Author was member of colonial government in Northern
Rhodesia. Argues for African rule and takes position
that federation was against African interests; presents
his account of formation and demise of Central African
Federation.

KEATLEY, Patrick
The Politics of Partnership: the Federation of Rhodesia
and Nyasaland (Harmondsworth, Middlesex: Penguin African Library, Penguin Books, 1963) 528 pp.
Bibliography.

Author wrote this book as Commonwealth correspondent of
'The Guardian'. Argues that present attitudes of Euro-

pean communities in Central Africa stem from those of
their predecessors (original British colonialists) and
that Britain had strong moral obligation to intervene in
political crisis in order to assure peaceful solution
which would include Africans in government and economy.

ROTBERG, Robert I.
The Rise of Nationalism in Central Africa: the making of
Malawi and Zambia, 1873-1964 (Cambridge, Mass.: Harvard
University Press, 1967)   360 pp.
Bibliography.

Seeks to understand reality of colonial rule in Malawi
and Zambia and nature of African response; to analyze
roots of African nationalism and its forms of expression;
to consider whether these expressions indicated existence
of widespread grievances or only aspirations of African
elite.

PIKE, John G.
Malawi: a political and economic history (London: Pall
Mall Press, 1968)   248 pp.
Bibliography.

Author served in colonial administration in Nyasaland.
Focuses on social, economic and political background to
most significant political dilemma in Malawi today: 'to
maintain its political independence and rapport with
African states of the north, all of which are opposed to
the white-dominated states south of the Zambezi River,
and at the same time to live with the accidents of history and geography that make it economically dependent
on the south'.

4. Rhodesia (Zimbabwe)

WINDRICH, Elaine
The Rhodesian Problem: a documentary record 1923-73
(London: Routledge & Kegan Paul, 1975)   312 pp.
Bibliography.

Documentary record covers period from establishment of
Crown colony in 1923 to illegal UDI in 1965 and post-
independence efforts to settle conflict. Documents
trace development of conflict between white minority
and black majority; illustrate methods used by Smith
regime to maintain effective power. Includes over 60
documents, covering many points of view.

YOUNG, Kenneth
    Rhodesia and Independence: a study in British colonial
    policy (London: J.M. Dent & Sons, Ltd., 1969) 684 pp.
    Bibliography.

    Thorough political history of Rhodesia from 1950, with
    introductory background to earlier development; is crit-
    ical of British policy -- discussion is based on substan-
    tial primary research. Appendices comprise various doc-
    uments related especially to UDI and negotiations.

5. South Africa

CARTER, Gwendolen M.
    The Politics of Inequality: South Africa since 1948
    (London: Thames & Hudson, 1958)   535 pp.
    Bibliography.

    Political history/analysis of South Africa since 1948
    when National Party took office. First four chapters
    study in detail Nationalist Party and nature of its gov-
    ernment; chapter five considers various opposition par-
    ties and their roles in political system; final chapter
    deals with South Africa's international relations. Ap-
    pendices relate mainly to election statistics and party
    programmes.

HEPPLE, Alex
    South Africa: a political and economic history (London:
    Pall Mall Press, 1966)   282 pp.
    Bibliography.

    Argues that real issue of race is, in fact, an economic
    one and that most of racial discrimination practised in
    South Africa has to do with exploitation of non-white
    labour.

HAIM, Ronald
    The Failure of South African Expansion 1908-1948 (London:
    Macmillan, 1972)   219 pp.
    Bibliography.

    Discusses political history of South Africa's unsuccess-
    ful attempts to extend union to Rhodesia, High Commis-
    sion Territories, etc. Useful background to less formal
    attempts made more recently to expand South African in-
    fluence.

KARIS, Thomas, and Gwendolen M. CARTER, eds.
> From Protest to Challenge: a documentary history of Afri-
> can politics in South Africa 1882-1964 (Stanford, Cal-
> if.: Hoover Institution Press, 1972-3) Three volumes.
> Bibliography.
>
> Vol. I: Protest and Hope, 1882-1934 (by Sheridan Johns)
> Vol. II: Hope and Challenge, 1935-52 (by Thomas Karis)
> Vol. III: Challenge and Violence, 1953-64 (forthcoming)
>
> Excellent collection (many documents are published for
> first time). Each section includes introduction by edi-
> tors, followed by relevant series of documents. Focuses
> on African political activity; includes some of joint
> efforts with whites, Indians and Coloureds, but does not
> deal with independent efforts of these groups.

SIMONS, H.J., and R.E. SIMONS
> Class and Colour in South Africa 1850-1950 (Harmonds-
> worth, Middlesex: Penguin African Library, Penguin Books,
> 1969)   702 pp.
> Bibliography.
>
> Written by two political activists against South African
> regime. Socio-political history and analysis of rise to
> power of white supremacist regime and of how and why it
> continues in power; study relates particularly to class
> struggle in South Africa and whether social classes co-
> incide with colour groups, and if so, what are effects
> in terms of African national liberation movement.

WILSON, Monica, and Leonard THOMPSON, eds.
> The Oxford History of South Africa: Volume II: South
> Africa 1870-1966 (Oxford: Clarendon Press, 1971) 584 pp.
> Bibliography.
>
> Of most direct interest to students of politics are sec-
> tions on subjection of African chiefdoms, Great Britain
> and Afrikaner Republics, Compromise of Union, Afrikaner
> nationalism, African nationalism and South Africa and
> modern world.

6. South West Africa (Namibia)

FIRST, Ruth
> South West Africa (Harmondsworth, Middlesex: Penguin
> African Library, Penguin Books, 1963)   264 pp.
> Bibliography.
>
> Stresses period from 1915 when South Africa took over
> South West Africa as League of Nations mandate; argues

that from beginning South West Africa was considered
and exploited by South Africa as a colony; discusses how
Africans were deprived of land, of political representa-
tion and of freedom to live and work where and how they
wished. Law section discusses evolution of South West
Africa issue at United Nations.

WELLINGTON, John H.
South West Africa and Its Human Issues (Oxford: Clarendon Press, 1967) 461 pp.

Large part of book concentrates on geographical setting
and African peoples of South West Africa; also provides
history of German colonialism. Part III discusses period of mandate, relationship with United Nations, institution of apartheid , and South Africa's attempts to
appease world opinion with its 'New Plan'.

8. Zambia

CAPLAN, Gerald L.
The Elites of Barotseland 1878-1969: a political history
of Zambia's western province (London: C. Hurst & Co.,
1970) 270 pp.
Bibliography.

Concerned with identifying changing locus of power in
Barotseland between 1878-1969, focuses on power struggle
among elite groups. Emphasizes consequences for this
African kingdom of an elite which tried to accommodate
European power and which preferred to ally itself with
white imperialists against African nationalists.

HALL, Richard
Zambia (London: Pall Mall Press, 1965) 357 pp.
Bibliography.

Political history of Zambia beginning with first arrival
of Europeans through 1965 and independence. Last chapter provides survey of economic history, especially regarding copperbelt. Concentrates on rise of African
nationalism during colonial period and on events leading
to independence.

MULFORD, David C.
Zambia: the politics of independence 1957-64 (London:
Oxford University Press, 1967) 362 pp.
Bibliography.

Studies constitutional change and development of African
nationalist political parties in Northern Rhodesia.

B. POLITICAL SYSTEMS, GOVERNMENT

POTHOLM, Christian P. and Richard DALE, eds.
Southern Africa in Perspective: essays in regional politics (New York: The Free Press, 1972)   418 pp. Bibliography.

Series of essays presenting various points of view on aspects of politics in Southern Africa; covers South Africa, South West Africa, Botswana, Lesotho, Swaziland, Angola, Mozambique, Rhodesia, Zambia, Malawi. Tries to establish patterns of political behaviour, both within each individual country and within region.

1. Botswana

YOUNG, B.A.
Bechuanaland (London: HMSO, 1966)   127 pp.

General survey of country - its political, social, economic aspects.

2. Lesotho

ASHTON, Hugh
The Basuto: a social study of traditional and modern Lesotho (International African Institute; London: Oxford University Press, 1967)   359 pp. Bibliography.

Author has synthesized all previously published material plus his own field work to produce all-round survey of Basuto people; additions for second edition emphasize impact of emergence of modern politics; basic emphasis of book is anthropological.

COATES, Austin
Basutoland (London: HMSO, 1966)   135 pp.

Presents general introduction to social, economic and political life in Basutoland.

SPENCE, J.E.
Lesotho: the politics of dependence (Institute of Race Relations; London: Oxford University Press, 1968) 88 pp.

Emphasizes geographical remoteness from independent Africa and economic dependence on South Africa as crucial influences on patterns of internal development and foreign relations.

4. Rhodesia

ARRIGHI, Giovanni
   The Political Economy of Rhodesia   (The Hague: Mouton,
   1967)   60 pp.
   Bibliography.

   Attempts to provide theoretical framework for analysis
   of forces which have shaped Rhodesian social system;
   framework is based on Marxist categories of economic
   base, class structure and superstructure.

BARBER, James
   Rhodesia: the road to rebellion   (Institute of Race Re-
   lations; London: Oxford University Press, 1967)   338 pp.
   Bibliography.

   Emphasizes conflict in political sphere during period
   1960-65; discusses break-up of Federation, 1961 constitution and referendum, 1962 election and triumph of
   Right and government under Rhodesian Front party.

BULL, Theodore, ed.
   Rhodesian Perspective   (London: Michael Joseph, 1967)
   184 pp.
   Bibliography.

   Author was involved with 'Central African Examiner', an
   independent journal of opinion, which was forced to close
   after UDI. Book is prepared with help of other contributors to 'Examiner' with intention of showing spectrum
   of Rhodesian life; discusses background to white politics, policy of separate development, education, economy
   and background to black politics; final chapter presents
   current attitudes of different racial groups.

CLEMENTS, Frank
   Rhodesia: the course to collision   (London: Pall Mall
   Press, 1969)   286 pp.
   Bibliography.

   Studies political and social development of Rhodesian
   colony which led to UDI; emphasizes evolution of attitudes and political alignments of population and discusses how 'African question' emerged from its status of
   being outside Rhodesian politics to become decisive
   issue.

MURRAY, D.J.
The Governmental System in Southern Rhodesia   (Oxford:
Clarendon Press, 1970)   393 pp.
Bibliography.

Emphasis on actual processes by which important policy
decisions are formulated, are accepted by relevant individuals and groups, are carried out; goal is to trace
regular relationships operating in society and to identify common patterns. Studies formal and informal structures and sectors of government.

O'MEARA, Patrick
Rhodesia: racial conflict or coexistence   (Ithaca, N.Y.:
Cornell University Press, 1975)   217 pp.
Bibliography.

Framework of analysis based on conflict theory; describes
different forms of pressure politics in context of racial
cleavage in Rhodesia; emphasizes current politics though
provides some background of historical development.

5. South Africa

ADAM, Heribert
Modernizing Racial Domination: South Africa's political
dynamics   (Berkeley/Los Angeles: University of California Press, 1971)   203 pp.
Bibliography.

Author stresses that he is trying to avoid tone of moral
indignation which is common in writings on South Africa.
Based on political economy analysis; describes 'pragmatic race oligarchy' and its effects; considers possible
means of bringing about change.

ADAM, Heribert, ed.
South Africa: sociological perspectives   (London: Oxford
University Press, 1971)   340 pp.
Bibliography (sources since 1960; over 30 pp.).

Authors all take critical position towards apartheid
but represent a variety of political viewpoints; essays
are interdisciplinary and attempt to analyze changing
interest structures which determine actions of South
African groups, both white and black.

BROOKES, Edgar H., ed.
Apartheid: a documentary study of modern South Africa
(London: Routledge & Kegan Paul, 1968)   228 pp.
Bibliography.

Editor lets documents speak for themselves in order to
define 'apartheid' and its implications for South African
society; various documents deal not only with meaning of
apartheid for South Africa as a whole, but also with its
implications for education and for churches and with
broader social consequences.

BUNTING, Brian
   The Rise of the South African Reich   (Harmondsworth,
   Middlesex: Penguin African Library, Penguin Books, 1964)
   332 pp.

   Author is South African journalist who was forced to
   leave for political reasons. Analyzes trend towards
   'fascism' of white supremacist government; discusses
   political thought of leaders of Nationalist Party and
   its affinity for Nazi party in Germany; describes government measures which have become increasingly repressive.

CARTER, Gwendolen, Thomas KARIS and Newell M. STULTZ
   South Africa's Transkei: the politics of domestic colon-
   ialism (London: Heinemann, 1967)   200 pp.
   Bibliography.

   Study of Transkei - a Bantustan, feature of South African
   policy of separate development. Critical appraisal of
   theory and practice of separate development; discusses
   politics and administration within Transkei and implications of Transkei situation for South Africa as a whole.

HAMMOND-TOOKE, W.D.
   Command or Consensus: the development of Transkeian
   local government (Cape Town: David Philip, 1975)   240 pp.
   Bibliography.

   Describes local government at three points in time: pre-
   colonial system of independent chiefdoms, period of direct rule under magistrates, new system of Bantu authorities. Deals with system, rather than politics as such;
   argues that leadership must be open to all on basis of
   ability and merit, not confined to holders of traditional
   offices.

HILL, Christopher R.
   Bantustans: the fragmentation of South Africa (Institute
   of Race Relations; London: Oxford University Press, 1964)
   114 pp.

   Discusses Bantustans (African Reserves) as they relate
   to theory and practice of apartheid or separate develop-

ment; describes recent developments in Transkei and
Natal in detail; discusses question of self-government
in Bantustans. Account of economics of Bantustans is
quite revealing about impracticality of Bantustan system.

HORRELL, Muriel
The African Homelands of South Africa (South African
Institute of Race Relations, Johannesburg, 1973) 176 pp.

General survey of homelands; includes substantial chapter on government and administration.

HORWITZ, Ralph
The Political Economy of South Africa (London: Weidenfeld & Nicolson, 1967) 522 pp.

Emphasizes role of political factor in modern economic
development of South Africa, in that it has been 'continuing instrument and occasion of action and reaction'.
But, author argues, that political factor has changed its
form over time although motivations have been constant:
political factor being control of South African society/
economy by whites i.e. political consciousness of Afri-
kanerdom.

LEFTWICH, Adrian, ed.
South Africa: economic growth and political change, with
comparative studies of Chile, Sri Lanka and Malaysia
(London: Allison & Busby, 1974) 357 pp.

Focuses on debate about relationship between economic
growth and socio-political change; most essays relate to
South Africa but others provide opportunity for comparative approach to theoretical issues.

THOMPSON, Leonard and Jeffrey BUTLER, eds.
Change in Contemporary South Africa (Berkeley: Univer-
sity of California Press, forthcoming)
Bibliography.

Sixteen essays by social scientists and historians on
different aspects of contemporary South Africa, with
introduction by Leonard Thompson.

VAN DEN BERGHE, Pierre
South Africa: a study in conflict (Berkeley/Los Angeles:
University of California Press, 1967) 371 pp.
Bibliography.

Sociological study of South Africa with conflict being
dominant theme. Includes historical background and broad
description of social structure.

6. South West Africa

SEGAL, Ronald and Ruth FIRST, eds.
South West Africa: travesty of trust   (London: Andre
Deutsch, 1967)   352 pp.

Expert papers and findings of International Conference
on South West Africa, Oxford, 23-26 March 1966, with
postscript by Iain MacGibbon on 1966 Judgement of International Court of Justice. Presents facts and arguments
related to position that South Africa has persistently
violated its 'trust' by its policy of race domination.

7. Swaziland

BARKER, Dudley
Swaziland (London: HMSO, 1965)   146 pp.

General survey of economic, social and political life of
Swazi people.

KUPER, Hilda
The Swazi: a South African kingdom   (New York: Rinehart
& Winston, 1963)   87 pp.
Bibliography.

Book deals with Swazi in years 1934-45 primarily, but is
relevant to study of politics of African kingdom. Final
chapter updates study; discusses trends of change and
continuity of tradition; in chapter on political structure, describes centralized state and dual monarchy.

POTHOLM, Christian P.
Swaziland: the dynamics of political modernization
(Berkeley/Los Angeles: University of California Press,
1972)   183 pp.
Bibliography.

Book analyzes traditional political system and how it
has been affected by emergence of modern politics; stresses continuing important role of monarchy; discusses relations between Swaziland and South Africa and prospects
for future.

8. Zambia

TORDOFF, William, ed.
Politics in Zambia   (Manchester: Manchester University
Press, 1974)   439 pp.
Bibliography.

Relates to politics in period 1964-72 and can be regarded as sequel to Mulford on 1957-64. Introduction gives

historical perspective and subsequent chapters discuss
various aspects of Zambian political system: sectionalism,
political parties, elections, government and administration, trade unionism, etc.

C. POLITICAL PARTIES, INTEREST GROUPS AND IDEOLOGIES

ANSARI, S.
    Liberation Struggle in Southern Africa: a bibliography
    of source material (Gurgaon, Haryana, India: Indian
    Documentation Service, 1972)   107 pp.

    1165 entries; author index; includes books, articles and
    documents on Namibia, Southern Rhodesia, former Portu-
    guese colonies.

GIBSON, Richard
    African Liberation Movements: contemporary struggles
    against white minority rule (Institute of Race Relations;
    London: Oxford University Press, 1972)   350 pp.
    Bibliography.

    Author is Afro-American correspondent and states his
    commitment to cause of black Africans. Book surveys
    contemporary African liberation movements; discusses po-
    litical history of each separately, by country: South
    Africa, South West Africa, Rhodesia, former Portuguese
    colonies, the Horn of Africa. Provides additional per-
    spective by examining political struggles within move-
    ments themselves and by discussing efforts at reformist
    solutions which preceded revolutionary action.

3. Malawi

MAIR, Lucy
    The Nyasaland Elections of 1961 (Institute of Common-
    wealth Studies, University of London; London: The Ath-
    lone Press, 1962)   87 pp.

    This election analysis provides background information,
    discusses preparations for elections, political parties
    participating in election, candidates, programmes and
    manifestos and campaign. Appendices include constitu-
    tion of Malawi Congress Party and of Christian Democrat-
    ic Party.

4. Rhodesia

BOWMAN, Larry W.
    Politics in Rhodesia: white power in an African state
    (Cambridge, Mass: Harvard University Press, 1973) 206 pp.

Bibliography.

Concerned with three different political interactions:
between white and black in Rhodesia, between local white
government and British government over limits of white
authority within Rhodesia, within white Rhodesian community itself over strategies to ensure continued white
domination.

MAXEY, Kees
The Fight for Zimbabwe: the armed conflict in Southern
Rhodesia since UDI (London: Rex Collings, 1975) 196 pp.

Traces armed conflict between African guerillas and Ian
Smith's white regime in Rhodesia; based primarily on
white Rhodesian sources because little has been published
by guerillas. Thus, nature of success may be understated.
Discusses strategies of nationalist groups, Rhodesian
security forces and military aid from South Africa.

5. South Africa

BENSON, Mary
South Africa: the struggle for a birthright (Harmondsworth, Middlesex: Penguin African Library, Penguin Books,
1966) 314 pp.
Bibliography.

Political history of African National Congress of South
Africa beginning in 1912.

DOXEY, G.V.
The Industrial Colour Bar in South Africa (London: Oxford University Press, 1961) 205 pp.

Provides general view of structure and stratification of
industrial labour market in South Africa and attempts to
isolate some of more important forces which have influenced its development since discovery of diamonds in
1870s; emphasizes legal rigidity in labour market.

FEIT, Edward
African Opposition in South Africa: the failure of pas-
sive resistance (Stanford, Calif.: The Hoover Institution, 1967) 223 pp.

Analysis relates to how failures of African National
Congress were due to factors other than merely 'odds'
against them. Analyzes, in particular, two campaigns
of ANC: 'Western Area' and 'Bantu Education' campaigns
in order to illustrate planning and organization in ANC.

FEIT, Edward
South Africa: the dynamics of the African National Congress (Institute of Race Relations; London: Oxford University Press, 1962)   73 pp.

Attempts to analyze why, despite grievances of Africans,
ANC failed to become an effective mass movement; particularly relates to attempted implementation of ANC's Programme of Action: non-violent non-cooperation; discusses
problems facing such a programme.

FIRST, Ruth, Jonathan STEELE and Christabel GURNEY
The South African Connection: Western investment in apartheid (London: Temple Smith, 1972)   352 pp.

Emphasizes interdependence of vested political and busi-
ness interests; argues that there is 'vast gulf between
liberal rhetoric and illiberal actions of advanced industrial societies'. Tries to explain continuing economic
involvement of Britain and other Western countries in
South Africa; asks whether industrialization is really
breaking down apartheid. Useful appendices concerning
British investors.

HEARD, Kenneth A.
General Elections in South Africa 1940-1970 (London:
Oxford University Press, 1974)   269 pp.

Period covered refers to that in which National Afrikan-
erdom established its political hegemony in South Africa.
Each chapter deals with particular election and broadly
follows same pattern: provide insights into relevant
circumstances surrounding each election; present major
issues of each campaign and parties' respective positions
on them; examine voters' responses to these issues and
policies.

KUPER, Leo
An African Bourgeoisie: race, class and politics in
South Africa (New Haven: Yale University Press, 1965)
452 pp.
Bibliography.

Discusses African perspectives on political change and
race relations; studies process of class differentiation
within African communities; studies occupational milieu,
institutional context and questions of tension and ad-
justment between institutional structures. Author takes
liberal point of view, keeping away from talk of violent
revolutionary change.

LERUMO, A.
Fifty Fighting Years: the Communist Party of South Africa 1921-71 (London: Inkululeko Publications, 1971)
216 pp.

A history cum evaluation of Communist Party, written for
its 50th anniversary. Emphasizes African resistance to
imperialism both in early and modern periods and in all
forms; discusses alliance between CP and African nationalist groups (from communist point of view). Appendices
contain documents related to various events in CP's
history.

LEWIN, Julius
Politics and Law in South Africa: essays on race relations (London: Merlin Press, 1963)   116 pp.

Series of essays with central theme: relative power of
Afrikaner nationalism, African nationalism and English
economic interests. Argues that Afrikaner nationalism
has triumphed because only two forces that might have
restrained it could not act in alliance with each other.

MAYER, Philip
Townsmen or Tribesmen: conservatism and the process of
urbanization in a South African city (Institute of So-
cial and Economic Research, Rhodes University; Cape
Town: Oxford University Press, 1961)   306 pp.
Bibliography.

Sociological study of Xhosa tribe in East London, South
Africa. Compares conservative section of tribe with
more progressive, westernized section in terms of behaviour patterns, attitudes and values as expressed in
and out of urban environment. Study is of particular
interest with regard to problems of labour migrancy and
policy related to labour. Considered the classic study
in its field.

MUNGER, Edwin S.
Afrikaner and African Nationalism: South African paral-
lels and parameters (Institute of Race Relations; London: Oxford University Press, 1967)   142 pp.

Introduction is actually bibliographical essay. Study
is comparative interpretation of two opposing nationalisms in South Africa. Starts from roots and carries
through to present; important point concerns failure or
lack of influence of English liberalism.

PATTERSON, Sheila
   The Last Trek: a study of the Boer people and the Afrikaner nation   (London: Routledge & Kegan Paul, 1957)
   336 pp.

   Traces historical development of Boer people from 'op-
   pressed nationhood to oppressive nationalism' and attempts
   to analyze real character of Boers/Afrikaners, going
   beyond conventional stereotypes. Book is still most relevant to current politics in South Africa.

POTTER, Elaine
   The Press as Opposition: the political role of South
   African newspapers   (London: Chatto & Windus, 1975)
   228 pp.
   Bibliography.

   Begins study in 1948 when Nationalist Party came to power and covers period to 1968.   Argues that English-lan-
   guage press was 'external' opposition, while Afrikaans-
   language press was, as institution within ranks of government, an 'internal' opposition; traces evolution of
   press, ownership of press, readership of press, restraints
   on press and relations between press and government.

ROBERTSON, Janet
   Liberalism in South Africa 1948-63   (Oxford: Clarendon
   Press, 1971)   252 pp.
   Bibliography.

   Studies those whites and blacks in South Africa who
   wanted to abolish racial discrimination and to extend
   equal rights to non-whites within existing parliamentary
   system, i.e. liberals.   Studied mainly through political
   parties and other political groupings and their evolution
   in recent South African history.

STULTZ, Newell M.
   Afrikaner Politics in South Africa 1934-48   (Berkeley/
   Los Angeles: University of California Press, 1974) 200 pp.
   Bibliography.

   Studies politics among white electorate of South Africa
   on basis of such concepts as political integration, politics of conciliation, political compromise, etc., in
   particular, as they affect Afrikaner community.

WALSHE, Peter
 The Rise of African Nationalism in South Africa: the
 African National Congress 1912-52 (London: C. Hurst &
 Co., 1970)   480 pp.
 Bibliography.

 Analyzes policies, political attitudes and organizational
 structures that characterized ANC from its foundation in
 1912 to its major confrontation with Afrikaner nationalism in Defiance Campaign of 1952. Described within context of modern, dynamic economy; emphasizes outward-
 looking nature of African nationalism because of Southern
 African context.

8. Zambia

BATES, Robert H.
 Unions, Parties and Political Development: a study of
 mineworkers in Zambia (New Haven: Yale University Press,
 1971)   291 pp.
 Bibliography.

 Analyzes attempts of Zambian government to constrain behaviour of African mineworkers in accord with its development objectives, especially government's use of union
 and party structures to regulate and control their behaviour. Provides insight into degree to which public policy prevails over private interest in African labour
 force.

MULFORD, David C.
 The Northern Rhodesia General Election 1962 (Nairobi:
 Oxford University Press, 1964; Oxford: Institute of
 Commonwealth Studies, 1964)   205 pp.
 Bibliography.

 Election study of first electoral confrontation between
 Africans and Europeans which produced first African government. Study emphasizes 1962 Constitution which en-
 couraged non-racial politics and describes its effect on
 campaigns and organization of main political parties

D. BIOGRAPHIES, MEMOIRS, SPEECHES, WRITINGS BY POLITICAL LEADERS

2. Lesotho

KHAKETLA, B.M.
 Lesotho, 1970: an African coup under the microscope
 (London: C. Hurst & Co., 1971)   350 pp.

88   The Politics of African and Middle Eastern States

Author has been prominent political figure in Lesotho.
Discussion centres on factors which led to political
crisis in Lesotho in 1970. Author's arguments are biased
in favour of government of King Moshoeshve II which was
deposed in 1970 by coup during first post-independence
elections; very critical of new government of Chief
Leabua Jonathan.

3. Malawi

SHORT, Philip
Banda (London: Routledge & Kegan Paul, 1974) 357 pp.
Bibliography.

Biography of Hastings Kamuzu Banda traces his education,
political involvement and development of his racial attitudes; describes his role in defeating Central African
Federation and in achieving independence for Malawi;
emphasizes Banda's alienation from other African leaders
and evolution of his conciliatory policies towards white-
dominated South Africa.

4. Rhodesia

KAPUNGU, Leonard T.
Rhodesia: the struggle for freedom (New York: Orbis
Books, 1974) 177 pp.

Empassioned account of Rhodesian political situation
before and after UDI; written by supporter of Zimbabwe
nationalist movement. Interesting discussion of dilemma of the churches in Rhodesia; last chapters consider
potential for revolution in Zimbabwe.

LARDNER-BURKE, Desmond
Rhodesia: the story of the crisis (London: Oldbourne,
1966) 101 pp.

Author was member of Ian Smith's cabinet; with forward
written by Smith. Book is his version of inside story
of negotiations which took place in latter half of 1965;
is firmly in support of Smith and his government; defends
Rhodesian system as progressive.

MTSHALI, B. Vulindlela
Rhodesia: background to conflict (New York: Hawthorn
Books, 1967) 255 pp.
Bibliography.

Author is South African Zulu and has close contacts with
nationalist movements and leaders. Sees conflict as

between European settler nationalism and black African
nationalism; refers to similarities in South Africa but
focuses on subjugation suffered by blacks in Rhodesia
and their attempts to 'redress wrongs done to them';
examines this process in historical, political, economic
and diplomatic terms.

SITHOLE, Ndabaningi
   African Nationalism (London: Oxford University Press,
   1968) Second edition. 196 pp.

First edition was justification of African nationalism.
Second edition attempts to explain how African nationalism has achieved its objectives as evidenced by emergence
of independent African countries. Part I is autobiogra-
phical: author has been leader of Rhodesian African nationalist movement and was at time of writing under
detention. Part II discusses factors contributing to
rise of African nationalism; Part III deals with nature
of white supremacy; Part IV deals with post-independence
problems.

5. South Africa

BENSON, Mary
   Chief Albert Lutuli of South Africa (London: Oxford
   University Press, 1963) 68 pp.
   Bibliography.

Biography of Chief Albert Lutuli describing his participation in African National Congress of South Africa and
his political activities of behalf of black South Africans which led him to win Nobel Peace Prize.

HANCOCK, W.K.
   Smuts: the sanguine years 1870-1919 (London: Cambridge
   University Press, 1962) 619 pp.
   Smuts: the fields of force 1919-50 (London: Cambridge
   University Press, 1968) 590 pp.
   Bibliography (both volumes).

Authoritative biography of Field Marshal Smuts; is also
history of South Africa in times of Smuts.

KADALIE, Clements
   My Life and the ICU: the autobiography of a black trade
   unionist in South Africa (London: Frank Cass & Co., Ltd.,
   1970) 230 pp.

Edited with introduction by Stanley Trapido. Kadalie was
founder of Industrial and Commercial Workers' Union of

Africa and its national secretary 1921-29 (first African
mass movement in South Africa). Trapido says that Kadalie rated his own contribution to political and social
life of South Africa very highly but says that much of
this high regard was, in fact, justified by impact of
ICU on later organizations.

LUTHULI, Albert
Let My People Go: an autobiography (London: Collins,
1962)   256 pp.

Autobiography of leader of banned African National Congress of South Africa.

MARQUARD, Leo
The Peoples and Policies of South Africa (London: Oxford
University Press, 1969)   Fourth edition. 266 pp.

Survey written by well-known South African. Includes
historical background, study of people, government, administration, colour bar, politics/parties, education,
religion and relations with neighbours. Emphasizes racial policies and relations between different racial
groups; offers one of best introductions to South African situation.

MBEKI, Govan
South Africa: the peasants' revolt (Harmondsworth, Middlesex: Penguin African Library, Penguin Books, 1964)
159 pp.

Author was leader of ANC in South Africa; imprisoned
with Mandela and others in 1962. Writes critical study
of workings of apartheid policy in African reserves,
especially Transkei; describes political and economic
aspects of apartheid; argues that common people of Transkei reject these policies and that South African government is only creating dilemmas for itself.

PATON, Alan
Hofmeyr (London: Oxford University Press, 1964)   545 pp.
Bibliography.

Biography of Jan Hendrik Hofmeyr, considered by many to
be 'conscience' of South Africa during his lifetime, and
served in Smuts' cabinet. Written by best known South
African writer; very insightful into character of men
who governed South Africa in those days.

ROUX, Edward
Time Longer than Rope: a history of the black man's
struggle for freedom in South Africa (Madison: University of Wisconsin Press, 1964)   469 pp.
Bibliography.

Both political history and political memoir. Author par-
ticipated in succession of political movements in South
Africa, including Communist Party. Book deals largely
with inter-war generation of African politics but also
provides earlier historical background.

8. Zambia

KAUNDA, Kenneth D.
Humanism in Zambia and a Guide to Its Implementation
(Lusaka: Zambia Information Services, 1968)   50 pp.

Outline of Zambian government ideology and proposed
means for its implementation, especially concerned with
role of ruling party.

KAUNDA, Kenneth D.
Zambia Shall Be Free (London: Heinemann, 1962)   202 pp.

Autobiography of Kaunda; presents his point of view regarding independence struggle in Zambia.

LEGUM, Colin, ed.
Zambia: independence and beyond - the speeches of Kenneth
Kaunda (London: Thomas Nelson & Sons, Ltd., 1966) 265 pp.

Speeches emphasize Kaunda's commitment to founding non-
racial society in Zambia; cover period from December 1962
to early 1966. Book seems to be intended as tribute to
Kaunda.

MACPHERSON, Fergus
Kenneth Kaunda of Zambia: the times and the man (Lusaka:
Oxford University Press, 1974)   478 pp.
Bibliography.

Biography of Kenneth Kaunda, President of Zambia, concentrates on period of independence struggle, relates life
of Kaunda to events of the day. Author is historian who
knows both Kaunda and Zambia well.

E. EXTERNAL RELATIONS

3. Malawi

MCMASTER, Carolyn
    Malawi: foreign policy and development (London: Julian
    Friedman Publishers Ltd., 1974)   246 pp.
    Bibliography.

    Study is in two parts: (1) pre-independence period and
    after 1953 as Federation of Rhodesia and Nyasaland: con-
    siders economic and political contacts that affected
    post-independence foreign policies; (2) post-independence
    period, after 1964: discusses objectives and development
    of foreign policy with reference to domestic political
    conditions and economic requirements, and extent and
    nature of interaction within international system. Con-
    centrates on seeing what foreign policy options are
    actually open to Malawi and basis for eventual choice.

4. Rhodesia

DAY, John
    International nationalism: the extra-territorial rela-
    tions of Southern Rhodesian African nationalists
    (London: Routledge & Kegan Paul, 1967)   143 pp.
    Bibliography.

    Explains how and why Rhodesian nationalist movements
    (African) have tried to combine internal with interna-
    tional pressure in their drive for self-government;
    gives concise political/historical analysis. In partic-
    ular, discusses links with British government, with
    international institutions and with other states in
    Africa. Argues that movement turned its attentions
    abroad because its agitation within Rhodesia had little
    impact on government.

GOOD, Robert C.
    UDI: the international politics of the Rhodesian rebel-
    lion (London: Faber & Faber, 1973)   368 pp.
    Bibliography.

    Author was American ambassador to Zambia from March 1965
    through December 1968. Contemporary history of events
    related to Rhodesian UDI which involved international
    politics, diplomacy and economic measures. Well-docu-
    mented account; author played little role in these ev-
    ents, therefore account is quite objective but with
    insights gained from his vantage point.

5. South Africa

AUSTIN, Dennis
Britain and South Africa   (Royal Institute of International Affairs; London: Oxford University Press, 1966)
191 pp.
Bibliography.

Attempts to evaluate extent of British interests in South
Africa, both political and economic, and degree to which
these interests are likely to influence British policies
towards South Africa.

BARBER, James
South Africa's Foreign Policy 1945-70   (London: Oxford
University Press, 1973)   325 pp.
Bibliography.

Study of foreign policy focuses on government policy-
makers and factors which influence them; emphasizes relationship between external and internal affairs of
South Africa. Notes contrast between diplomatic and
economic contacts of international relations.

GRUNDY, Kenneth W.
Confrontation and Accommodation in Southern Africa: the
limits of independence (Berkeley/Los Angeles: University
of California Press, 1973)   360 pp.
Bibliography.

Study focuses on intra-regional patterns of international relations; includes discussion of nature of economic,
political, diplomatic relations. Author tries to emphasize areas of relevance which have been slighted in
other studies.

HAILEY, Lord
The Republic of South Africa and the High Commission
Territories (London: Oxford University Press, 1963)
136 pp.

Territories refer to British dependencies of Bechuanaland, Basutoland and Swaziland. Discusses political
status of these territories in relation to Britain and
to Union of South Africa; particular emphasis on South
Africa's efforts to have these territories incorporated
into Union. Although we know this never succeeded, this
study provides insights into current relations.

HANCE, William, ed.
　　Southern Africa and the United States (New York: Colum-
　　bia University Press, 1968)   171 pp.
　　Bibliography.

　　Four essays: (1) Vernon McKay: Southern Africa and its
　　implications for American policy; (2) Edwin Munger:
　　New white politics in South Africa; (3) Leo Kuper: Poli-
　　tical situation of non-whites in South Africa; (4) Wil-
　　liam Hance: The case for and against US disengagement
　　from South Africa. Authors are cautious in predicting
　　major political change within South Africa; all agree
　　that US pressure should not be relaxed though they do
　　differ as to exact policy proposals.

LEGUM, Colin and Margaret
　　South Africa: crisis for the West (London: Pall Mall
　　Press, 1964)   333 pp.
　　Bibliography.

　　Argue that racial crisis in South Africa will not be
　　resolved without international intervention; book is
　　directed at Western opinion and leadership because it is
　　Western countries which are most hesitant to intervene.

NOLUTSHUNGU, Sam C.
　　South Africa in Africa: a study in ideology and foreign
　　policy (Manchester: Manchester University Press, 1975)
　　329 pp.
　　Bibliography.

　　Divided into two parts: South Africa in colonial Africa
　　and South Africa in post-colonial Africa; argues that
　　it was object of South African policy to secure an opti-
　　mal organizational and ideological milieu in Africa;
　　therefore, South Africa tried to gain influence with
　　colonial powers and to persuade them to retain their
　　colonies. Post-colonial policy consists in trying to
　　end South Africa's isolation in Africa by offering aid
　　and trade to African governments. Deals mainly with
　　period 1945-71.

SPENCE, J.E.
　　Republic Under Pressure: a study of South African for-
　　eign policy (Chatham House Essays No. 9; London: Oxford
　　University Press, 1965)   132 pp.

　　Discusses relationship between domestic and foreign pol-
　　icy and also probable effect of external pressures on
　　South African government.

6. South West Africa

Ethiopia and Liberia versus South Africa: an official
account of the contentious proceedings on South West
Africa before the International Court of Justice at the
Hague 1960-66 (Pretoria: Department of Information)
304 pp.

Book is basically defense of South African position;
argues that court decision was favourable to South Africa and therefore stresses its importance.

IMISHUE, R.W.
South West Africa: an international problem   (Institute
of Race Relations; London: Pall Mall Press, 1965) 80 pp.
Bibliography.

Book intended to provide background of mandate leading
up to judgement of International Court of Justice. Appendices include texts of UN documents.

SLONIM, Solomon
South West Africa and the United Nations: an international mandate in dispute (Baltimore, Md.: Johns Hopkins University Press, 1973)   409 pp.
Bibliography.

Provides historical background, traces manner in which
dispute arose between South Africa and UN over international accountability for South West Africa; studies UN
efforts to unilaterally exercise supervisory authority
over territory; discusses role and decisions of Court;
finally, examines UN revocation of mandate and conse-
quent confrontation between UN and South Africa. Appendices include texts of relevant documents.

8. Zambia

HALL, Richard
The High Price of Principles: Kaunda and the white south
(New York: Africana Publishing Corp., 1970; London:
Hodder & Stoughton, 1969)   256 pp.

Discusses political situation inside Zambia since independence, role of Rhodesian problems as they affect
Zambia and vice-versa, and Zambia's relations with other
states of southern Africa. Argues that trend up to
1969 had put Kaunda in tenuous position, especially
since Rhodesian situation does still not appear near
resolution.

WEST AFRICA

A. POLITICAL HISTORY

AMIN, Samir
> L'Afrique de l'Ouest Bloquee: l'economie politique de la colonisation 1880-1970 (Paris: Editions de Minuit, 1971) 322 pp.
>
> Neo-colonialism in West Africa (Harmondsworth, Middlesex: Penguin African Library, Penguin Books, 1973) Bibliography.
>
> Has economic orientation; thesis is that economic problems of Africa today result from colonization and balkanization that took place in 19th century.

COHEN, William B.
> Rulers of Empire: the French colonial service in Africa (Stanford, Calif.: Hoover Institution Press, 1971) 279 pp. Bibliography.
>
> Emphasizes administration in French West Africa; study of French colonial administration, particularly of men who worked in it, their backgrounds, training and ideological outlook.

CROWDER, Michael
> West Africa Under Colonial Rule (London: Hutchinson & Co., Ltd., 1968) 540 pp.
>
> Comparative study of different impact of French and British colonial rule on West Africans and their reaction to it, covering period 1885-1945. Discusses colonial occupation and administrations, colonial economies, social change and origins of African politics.

HARGREAVES, John D.
> West Africa: the former French states (Englewood Cliffs, N.J.: Prentice-Hall, 1967) 183 pp. Bibliography.
>
> Study includes those countries which until 1958 formed part of AOF (Afrique Occidentale Francaise): Dahomey, Guinea, Ivory Coast, Mali, Mauritania, Niger, Senegal, Upper Volta, Togo. Examines broad themes of West African history; emphasizes colonial period under French rule.

MARSHALL, D. Bruce
The French Colonial Myth and Constitution-Making in the
Fourth Republic (New Haven: Yale University Press, 1973)
363 pp.
Bibliography.

'Myth' refers to vision held by French elite of an in-
dissoluble link between French and colonies; analyzes
deliberations of Constituent Assemblies (1945-6) in
France and factors that shaped their decisions; leads to
understanding of role of myth in determining French approach to decolonization.

MORTIMER, Edward
France and the Africans 1944-60: a political history
(London: Faber & Faber, 1969)   390 pp.

Studies, step-by-step, process leading to France grant-
ing independence to its colonies; very useful chronological study.

POST, Ken
The New States of West Africa (Harmondsworth, Middlesex:
Penguin African Library, Penguin Books, 1968)   231 pp.
Bibliography.

Basically concerned with process of decolonization, in
particular with results of duality of intention of colonial powers which at same time as they handed over political control to new rulers had no desire to give up
their economic stakes in these countries. Author studies
different effects and national responses to this situation.

THOMPSON, Virginia, and Richard ADLOFF
French West Africa (London: George Allen & Unwin, 1958)
626 pp.
Bibliography.

Useful reference for pre-independence period.

1. Benin (Dahomey)

CORNEVIN, Robert
Le Dahomey (Paris: Presses Universitaires de France,
1965)   128 pp.
Bibliography.

Concerns mainly pre-colonial and colonial periods; only
very brief consideration of post-independence until 1964.
Longer sections on economic and socio-religious life.

3. Gambia

GAILEY, Harry A., Jr.
A History of the Gambia (London: Routledge & Kegan Paul,
1964) 244 pp.
Bibliography.

Presents political development of Gambia; argues that
Gambia shows in microcosm most of problems facing any
new state; considers whether Gambia is viable state.
Especially notes dependence of Gambian economy on export
of groundnuts and considers its economic/political effects.

4. Ghana

AUSTIN, Dennis
Politics in Ghana 1946-60 (Royal Institute of International Affairs; London: Oxford University Press, 1970)
459 pp.
Bibliography.

Political history covering period from introduction of
first post-war constitution to inauguration of republic.
In particular, emphasizes results of three elections which
took place in 1951, 1954, 1956.

KIMBLE, David
A Political History of Ghana: the rise of Gold Coast nationalism 1850-1928 (Oxford: Clarendon Press, 1963)
587 pp.

Argues that Gold Coast nationalism had relatively early
origins. Book intended as historical case study of nationalism as it developed in one colony; argues that
there was essential continuity of development as centre
of loyalty of movements shifted from small independent
state or tribe to confederacy of states (Ashanti) or
wider ethnic or linguistic group (Akans); argues that
nationalism must be regarded primarily as reaction, not
spontaneous political force.

STANILAND, Martin
The Lions of Dagbon: political change in northern Ghana
(London: Cambridge University Press, 1975) 241 pp.
Bibliography.

Political history of Dagomba kingdom in northern Ghana;
examines policies used by colonial and national governments to preserve, exploit and assimilate pre-colonial
structure of authority; considers changes in local politics which have come about through action of external
authorities; case study of Yendi dispute.

WALLERSTEIN, Immanuel
The Road to Independence: Ghana and the Ivory Coast
(Paris/The Hague: Mouton, 1964)   200 pp.
Bibliography.

Social change under colonial rule studies, with particular reference to voluntary associations and relation of
elites to rise of nationalism; argues that although these
two countries were ruled by different colonial powers,
this difference fades in significance with time.

5. Guinea

AMEILLON, B.
La Guinee: bilan d'une independance   (Paris: Francois
Maspero, 1964)   210 pp.

Discusses Guinea's experience in struggle against colonialism: diminish role of institution of 'chefferie' as
agent of colonialists, breaking off of colonial ties
with French communaute, resultant economic revolution,
Guinea and relations with world.

7. Liberia

MARINELLI, Lawrence A.
The New Liberia: a historical and political survey
(London: Pall Mall Press, 1964)   244 pp.
Bibliography.

Brief introduction by L.S. Senghor. First half of book
is survey of Liberian political history including discussion of Tubman's rise to power, Open Door investment
policy, situation of health/education/economy and role
of Liberia in African affairs. Second half is series of
appendices especially documents, speeches, letters of
President Tubman, Liberian Constitution, etc.

10. Nigeria

COLEMAN, James S.
Nigeria: background to nationalism   (Berkeley/Los Angel-
es: University of California Press, 1963)   510 pp.
Bibliography.

Political history; focuses on background of emergence of
nationalism in Nigeria, covers period 1900-52. Analyzes
processes of social/political change which have created
situations leading to Nigerian peoples' nationalism.

OLUSANYA, G.O.
The Second World War and Politics in Nigeria 1939-53
(University of Lagos; London/Ibadan: Evans Bros. Ltd.,
1973)   181 pp.
Bibliography.

Studies effects of Nigerian participation on behalf of
British in World War II on nationalist movement in Nigeria after war; argues that ferment produced by war resulted in great political awakening in Nigeria - led to destruction of 'white man's myth', to higher consciousness
of racial discrimination and of principle of self-determination.

WHITAKER, C.S., Jr.
The Politics of Tradition: continuity and change in
Northern Nigeria 1946-66 (Princeton, N.J.: Princeton
University Press, 1970)   563 pp.
Bibliography.

Argues that data concerning experience of political
change in period dealt with does not confirm hypothesis
derived from conceptualization of change as modernization;
in other words, conceiving of process of change in 'confrontation' societies in terms of unavoidable choice between certain incompatible norms of behaviour is quest-
ionable; author describes some circumstances in Northern
Nigeria which might contradict these assumptions.

11. Senegal

CROWDER, Michael
Senegal: a study of French assimilation policy (London:
Methuen & Co., Ltd., 1967) Second edition. 151 pp.
Bibliography.

Studies Senegal as exception in terms of French colonial
policy: differentiates between policy of association
applied to other colonies and that of assimilation applied to Senegal. Approach is basically study of race
relations in their political manifestations and its long
term effects on Senegalese.

JOHNSON, G. Wesley, Jr.
The Emergence of Black Politics in Senegal: the struggle
for power in the four communes 1900-20 (Stanford, Calif.:
Stanford University Press, 1971)   260 pp.

Study describes political struggle between French colonial officials, French colonists, Creoles and indigenous

Senegalese for power in local political affairs. Senegalese case was probably unique in that African indigenous community did eventually gain considerable political
rights; gives insight into French colonial policy.

12. Sierra Leone

CARTWRIGHT, John R.
Politics in Sierra Leone 1947-67   (Toronto: University
of Toronto Press, 1970)   296 pp.
Bibliography.

Attempts to explain what enabled Sierra Leone to maintain a competitive political system and to resist formation of one-party or no-party system; emphasizes nature
of dominant oligarchy, form of its political organization and pressures from outside oligarchy in support of
pluralist system; argues that tribal/regional conflicts
brought about destruction of this system in 1967 with
military coup.

KUP, A.P.
Sierra Leone: a concise history   (Newton Abbot, Devon:
David & Charles, 1975)   272 pp.
Bibliography.

Chapter on modern political and constitutional change is
most relevant; because of broad coverage attempted by
author, book tends to be superficial in its analysis
and is largely descriptive; considerable material on
tribal composition of Sierra Leone.

B. POLITICAL SYSTEMS, GOVERNMENT

LEWIS, W. Arthur
Politics in West Africa   (The Whidden Lectures for 1965;
London: George Allen & Unwin, 1965)   90 pp.

Focuses on single-party system in West African context;
discusses its merits in terms of several issues such as
economic policy-making, international relations especially with former colonial powers, federalism, and
structure of system itself.   Gives broad introductory
coverage.

LEWIS, William H., ed.
French-Speaking Africa: the search for identity   (New
York: Walker & Co., 1965)   256 pp.

Book emerged from colloquium conducted in Washington,
D.C. in August 1964 under auspices of US Department of

State, Ford Foundation, Georgetown University and Afri-
can-American Institute. Articles on politics, social
and cultural situation, economics, foreign relations.

LLOYD, Peter C.
   Africa in Social Change: changing traditional societies
   in the modern world (Harmondsworth, Middlesex: Penguin
   Books, 1967)   363 pp.
   Bibliography.

   Relates to West Africa - both anglo- and francophone.
   Introduction to nature of African societies, traditional
   and modern elites, and social impact of 20th century
   contact with West. Appendix provides comparative data
   on states discusses.

LUSIGNAN, Guy de
   French-Speaking Africa Since Independence (London: Pall
   Mall Press, 1969)   416 pp.
   Bibliography (largely European sources).

   Tries to show how and why French policy was pushed towards decolonization (from French point of view); discusses French/African relations but does not recognize
   dangers of neocolonialism resulting from aid-trade relations and also from francophile elite.

SY, Seydou Madani
   Recherches sur l'Exercice du Pouvoir Politique en Afrique
   Noire (Cote d'Ivoire, Guinee, Mali) (Paris: Pedone, 1965)
   230 pp.

   Comparative political systems based on French legalistic
   school of analysis.

WRAITH, Ronald
   Local Administration in West Africa (London: George
   Allen & Unwin, 1972) Revised edition. 236 pp.

   Refers only to anglophone West Africa. Part I provides
   framework for study of local government/administration:
   decentralization, ecology of local government, function
   of local government, local authorities and personnel,
   party politics in local government and revenue of local
   authorities. Part II outlines situation in West African
   cities in Sierra Leone, Ghana, Nigeria. Argues that
   in period 1966-71 there was revival of central administration authority over local government; other trend is
   to restrict future activities of elected councillors
   because of their corruption and inefficiency in past.

1. Benin (Dahomey)

GLELE, Maurice A.

La Republique du Dahomey (Encyclopedie Politique et Constitutionnelle; Paris: Berger-Levrault, 1969) 73 pp. Bibliography.

Short, concise introduction to sociological setting, political and constitutional evolution in Dahomey; includes text of 1968 constitution and other documents.

GLELE, Maurice A.

Naissance d'un Etat Noir: l'evolution politique et constitutionnelle du Dahomey, de la colonisation a nos jours (Paris: Librairie General du Droit et Jurisprudence, R. Pichon and R. Durand-Auzias, 1969)

More comprehensive work by above author.

NZONGOLA, Georges

Essai sur le Dahomey (Brussels: Centre d'Etudes et de Documentation Africaine, 1971) Bibliography.

2. Cameroon

BENJAMIN, Jacques

Les Camerounais Occidentaux: la minorite dans un etat bicommunautaire (Montreal: Les Presses de l'Universite de Montreal, 1972) 250 pp. Bibliography.

Studies the cultural-based political conflicts in Cameroon and their implications for future of federal system; considers federalism as process in constant state of evolution; in particular, considers effects of federal institutions on 'Camerounais occidentaux', i.e. those in formerly British Cameroon.

BOCKEL, Alain

L'Administration Camerounaise (Encyclopedie Administrative; Paris: Berger-Levrault, 1971) 62 pp.

Monograph basically describes system of administration in Cameroon; is particularly interesting as study of federal administration, especially because of remnants of both French and British colonial administration systems. Includes documents relating to this administration.

GONIDEC, P.F.
    La Republique Federale du Cameroun   (Encyclopedie Poli-
    tique et Constitutionnelle; Paris: Editions Berger-
    Levrault, 1969)   86 pp.
    Bibliography.

    Description of Cameroon society and analysis of political
    and constitutional development - including discussion of
    various political forces and interest groups. Appendices
    provide texts of documents such as federal constitution
    and those of two parts of federation (East and West).

IMBERT, Jean
    Le Cameroun   (Paris: Presses Universitaires de France,
    1973)   126 pp.
    Bibliography.

    Discusses social, cultural, geographic, political and
    economic characteristics of Cameroon; particularly inter-
    esting because Cameroon is at junction in Africa of var-
    ious peoples and remnants of colonial powers and can be
    studied almost as mini-Africa.

JOHNSON, Willard R.
    The Cameroun Federation: political integration in a
    fragmentary society   (Princeton, N.J.: Princeton Univer-
    sity Press, 1970)   426 pp.
    Bibliography.

    Concentrates study on foundations of unity and on pro-
    gress made towards real political integration; uses both
    integration (functional) and conflict-focused analysis,
    i.e. continuities and discontinuities which emerge
    through process of 'development'.

KOM, David
    Le Cameroun: essai d'analyse economique et politique
    (Paris: Editions Sociales, 1971)   334 pp.
    Bibliography.

    Marxist analysis of political/economic situation of
    Africa by means of example of Cameroon; analyzes class
    struggle, fundamental structure of Cameroon economy and
    Cameroon economy in world context, leading up to pro-
    gramme for non-capitalist development.

LEVINE, Victor T.
The Cameroon Federal Republic   (Ithaca, N.Y.: Cornell University Press, 1971)   205 pp.
Bibliography.

General introduction to politics of Cameroon and its legacy from both French and British administrative systems; discusses problems arising from factions, economic diversity among regions, tribal rivalries, etc.

RUBIN, Neville
Cameroun: an African federation   (London: Pall Mall Press, 1971)   259 pp.
Bibliography.

Traces process leading to formation of federation and outlines institutions and policies identified with new state during its first ten years; strengths and weaknesses of federal system.   Appendices include various documents: mandates, trusteeships, constitution, etc.

3. Gambia

ARMAND-PREVOST, Michel
La Republique de Gambie   (Encyclopedie Politique et Constitutionnelle; Paris: Editions Berger-Levrault, 1973) 67 pp.
Bibliography.

Provides introduction to Gambian society; outlines evolution from British colony to independence in 1965, and from constitutional monarchy to republic in 1970. Discusses political forces, political parties, unions and foreign influences, and describes structure of republic. Appendices include text of constitution and other documents.

4. Ghana

APTER, David E.
Ghana in Transition   (Princeton, N.J.: Princeton University Press, 1972)   Second revised edition.   434 pp.

Treats problems of political institutional transfer; argues that Ghana, post-independence, was unable to maintain necessary degree of political stability because it lacked sufficient resources for genuine transformation of socio-economic infrastructure; Apter's study is of particular interest because he has followed up his original study and conclusions with new insights.

DUNN, John, and A.F. ROBERTSON
  Dependence and Opportunity: political change in Ahafo
  (London: Cambridge University Press, 1973)   400 pp.

  Study of political transformation on local level in
  Ahafo, Ghana. Studies period 1968-71 (based on original
  research) during which new constitution was approved and
  authority was handed over to Dr. Busia's elected government; studies election campaign, formation of new political allegiances, legitimization of new system in tradi-
  tional/historical context of Ahafo.

FITCH, Bob, and Mary OPPENHEIMER
  Ghana: end of an illusion (New York: Monthly Review
  Special Issue, Vol. 18, No. 3 (July-August 1966)) 144 pp.

  Analysis of background to coup which overthrew Nkrumah
  in Ghana in 1966, from point of view of historical mater-
  ialism i.e. class analysis and historical analysis. In
  particular, studies question of why coup failed to pro-
  voke any popular resistance, and how Nkrumah government
  had become so isolated from people despite its socialist
  policies.

FOSTER, Philip, and Aristide R. ZOLBERG, eds.
  Ghana and the Ivory Coast: perspectives on modernization
  (Chicago: University of Chicago Press, 1971)   303 pp.

  Series of essays providing comparative analysis of Ghana
  and Ivory Coast in spheres of politics, administration,
  law, education and economics. Objective of this explor-
  atory study is to obtain hypotheses towards theory of
  social change.

GENOUD, Roger
  Nationalism and Economic Development in Ghana (New York:
  Praeger, 1969)   244 pp.
  Bibliography.

  Interdisciplinary study of Ghana's development strategy
  during Nkrumah years; considers both economic and political problems and performance; covers period 1951-66.

LEVINE, Victor T.
  Political Corruption: the Ghana case (Stanford, Calif.:
  Hoover Institution Press, 1975)   169 pp.
  Bibliography.

  Specifically, studies unscheduled, unsanctioned use of
  public political resources and/or goods for private
  ends; meant as case study with wider implications.

OWUSU, Maxwell
   Uses and Abuses of Political Power: a case study of con-
   tinuity and change in the politics of Ghana   (Chicago:
   University of Chicago Press, 1970)   364 pp.
   Bibliography.

   Study of national integration, of social, economic and
   political unification in Ghana as seen through development of people of Swedru in Agona area of south-central
   Ghana; study covers period from end of 17th century to
   1966; concentrates on how traditional political institutions, symbolized by rule of chief and his elder-council-
   lors, have adapted or failed to adapt to changing environment of Eurocolonial domination, decolonization and of
   one-party state.

PINKNEY, Robert
   Ghana Under Military Rule 1966-69   (London: Methuen &
   Co., Ltd., 1972)   182 pp.
   Bibliography.

   Case study of operation of military government: assets
   and weaknesses as compared with their counterparts head-
   ing civilian administrations; studies questions of power,
   legitimacy, policy-making and implementation, etc.

WORONOFF, Jon
   West African Wager: Houphouet versus Nkrumah   (Metuchen,
   N.J.: The Scarecrow Press, Inc., 1972)   357 pp.
   Bibliography.

   Attempt to make comparative evaluation of Ivory Coast
   and Ghana in their political/economic development since
   1957; based on wager between Houphouet and Nkrumah.
   Compares independence and struggle for power, foreign
   policy, economic development, daily life; especially interesting comparison of two leaders and their personal
   impact on their respective countries.

5. Guinea

CHARLES, Bernard
   La Republique de Guinee   (Encyclopedie Politique et Constitutionnelle; Paris: Editions Berger-Levrault, 1972)
   69 pp.
   Bibliography.

   Discusses socio-political and constitutional evolution
   of Guinea and studies condition of contemporary political
   life.   Appendices provide documents including constitution and statutes of PDG.

DECKER, Henry de
  <u>Nation et Developpement Communautaire en Guinee et au</u>
  <u>Senegal</u> (Paris/The Hague: Mouton, 1967)   470 pp.
  Bibliography.

  Studies means used in Guinea and Senegal of achieving
  mass participation in political system and in process of
  development. Evaluates two separate models of community
  development: their ideological bases, their organization,
  their effects on mentality of people.

RIVIERE, Claude
  <u>Mutations Sociales en Guinee</u> (Paris: Editions Marcel
  Riviere et Cie., 1971)   418 pp.

  Studies problems involved in surmounting ethnic and
  other conflicts in modernizing society; from political
  point of view considers problem of stability of regime
  which has accelerated mutation/disequilibrium of behaviour and attitudes.

SURET-CANALE, Jean
  <u>La Republique de Guinee</u> (Paris: Editions Sociales, 1970)
  431 pp.
  Bibliography.

  From Marxist point of view, mainly concerned with socio-
  economic structures of Guinea, but also discusses political evolution from 1956-68.

6. Ivory Coast

COHEN, Michael A.
  <u>Urban Policy and Political Conflict in Africa: a study of</u>
  <u>the Ivory Coast</u> (Chicago: University of Chicago, 1974)
  262 pp.
  Bibliography.

  Studies relationships between public policy, social stratification and political conflict; based on field studies
  of three towns to determine consequences of urban policy
  on socio-economic and political life, but is concerned
  with national political processes.

MOURGEON, Jacques
  <u>La Republique de Cote d'Ivoire</u> (Encyclopedie Politique
  et Constitutionnelle; Paris: Editions Berger-Levrault,
  1969)   45 pp.
  Bibliography.

  Brief introduction to society and political system. Includes text of constitution and lists other documents.

7. Liberia

LIEBENOW, J.G.
Liberia: the evolution of privilege (Ithaca, N.Y.: Cornell University Press, 1969)   247 pp.
Bibliography.

Discusses existence and nature of Americo-Liberian elite which completely dominates political/economic system. Argues that although Liberia has achieved world prestige and high economic growth, majority of population have benefitted little or not at all; sees it as potentially explosive situation.

TIXIER, Gilbert
La Republique du Liberia (Encyclopedie Politique et Constitutionnelle; Paris: Editions Berger-Levrault, 1970) 47 pp.
Bibliography.

Outlines demographic, economic and cultural factors in socio-political system; discusses political/constitutional evolution in terms of executive, legislative and judicial branches of government; discusses political forces such as single political party, unions and social classes. Includes text of constitution.

8. Mali

HOPKINS, Nicholas S.
Popular Government in an African Town: Kita, Mali (Chicago: University of Chicago Press, 1972)   246 pp.
Bibliography.

Political anthropology on micro level; studies relative roles of local political participation in Kita and of state party bureaucracy in creating structure of political system; focuses on post-independence period.

JOUVE, Edmond
La Republique du Mali (Encyclopedie Politique et Constitutionnelle; Paris: Editions Berger-Levrault, 1974) 97 pp.
Bibliography.

Provides outline of Mali society, of its political and constitutional evolution as state, of national political forces and current political situation following coup d'etat of 1968. Appendices include texts of some important documents.

MEGAHED, Horeya T.
  Socialism and Nation-Building in Africa: the case of
  Mali 1960-68 (Budapest: Hungarian Academy of Sciences,
  Centre for Afro-Asian Research, 1970)   41 pp.

  Studies nature of 'socialism' in Mali context both in
  ideological terms and in practice; final section on problems of non-alignment and foreign aid for a socialist
  developing country.

10. Nigeria

ABERNATHY, David B.
  The Political Dilemma of Popular Education: an African
  case (Stanford, Calif.: Stanford University Press, 1969)
  357 pp.
  Bibliography.

  Case study of southern Nigeria intended to show relationship between education and political development in new
  nation; argues that southern Nigeria's educational policies lowered government's capacity to achieve its goals,
  introduced new inequalities and provided basis for new
  political and social cleavages.

ADEDEJI, Adebayo, ed.
  Nigerian Administration and its Political Setting (In-
  stitute of Administration, University of Ife, Nigeria;
  London: Hutchinson Educational Ltd., 1968)   162 pp.

  Contributions written largely by Nigerian administrators.
  Various points of view on interaction between politics
  and administration in terms of interest groups, civil
  service bureaucracy, public corporations and political
  process itself; all based on fact that professional politicians played direct role in administration.

ARIKPO, Okoi
  The Development of Modern Nigeria (Harmondsworth, Middlesex: Penguin African Library, Penguin Books, 1967)
  176 pp.
  Bibliography.

  Book written before Nigerian civil war, but is concerned
  with just those problems which eventually led to conflict:
  corruption, tribalism, factionalism. Concerned with
  history of formation of Nigeria as federal state and
  crisis of unity which followed.

AWA, Eme O.
Federal Government in Nigeria (Berkeley/Los Angeles:
University of California Press, 1964)   249 pp.
Bibliography.

Analyzes foundations of federalism in Nigeria, organization, powers and functions of federal and regional governments respectively, and discusses unsettled problems
of federalism such as fears of minorities and case for
more regions.

BAKER, Pauline H.
Urbanization and Political Change: the politics of Lagos
1917-67 (Berkeley/Los Angeles: University of California
Press, 1974)   384 pp.
Bibliography.

Examines impact of urbanization on politics in Lagos -
tropical Africa's largest city. Focuses on role of African urban poor, formation of community power structure
in non-Western environment and dynamics of modernization
in developing city.

BLITZ, L. Franklin, ed.
The Politics and Administration of Nigerian Government
(London: Sweet & Maxwell, 1965; Lagos: African Universi-
ties Press, 1965)   281 pp.
Bibliography.

Series of essays providing introduction to Nigerian government as it existed before civil war; outlines historical background, tribal composition, constitutional development, structure of government at federal level, at
regional level and at local level, political parties,
courts and legal system, maintenance of public order,
higher public service, foreign relations.

BRETTON, Henry L.
Power and Stability in Nigeria: the politics of decolon-
ization (New York: Praeger, 1962)
Bibliography.

Focuses on political stability as most critical factor
in decolonization and in Nigeria's national survival;
argues that economic development takes place under general control and supervision of political forces, that
choices are made on political grounds, and that in decolonization process, political 'kingdom' precedes economic one.

MACKINTOSH, John P.
Nigerian Government and Politics: prelude to the revolution (Evanston, Ill.: Northwestern University Press,
1966; London: George Allen & Unwin, 1966)   651 pp.
Bibliography.

Author plus five other contributors provide analysis of
evolution of federal system of government and discuss
several political events or groups in order to provide
understanding of how political machinery works; includes
analysis of political parties and election trends and of
balance of power between regions. In particular, concerned with effectiveness of governmental institutions inherited from British administration.

MELSON, Robert, and Howard WOLPE, eds.
Nigeria: modernization and the politics of communalism
(Michigan State University Press, 1971)   680 pp.

Series of essays related to political question of 'how
to reconcile the demands of communal groups for security
and autonomy with the requirements of the nation-state
for order and unity'. Takes theoretical approach to case
study of Nigeria; argues that perhaps conflict actually
produces tribalism, rather than vice-versa. Authors of
essays are known scholars of Nigerian affairs.

PANTER-BRICK, S.K., ed.
Nigerian Politics and Military Rule: prelude to the
civil war (Institute of Commonwealth Studies; London:
Athlone Press, 1970)   276 pp.

In two parts: (1) collection of essays related to developments in Nigeria leading to outbreak of civil war;
attempt to provide understanding of how and why secession was declared (authors include P.C. Lloyd, A.R.
Luckham, M.J. Dent, B.J. Dudley, K. Whiteman, P.F. Daw-
son); (2) summary analysis of documentary material including selected decrees and speeches, etc.

POST, Kenneth, and Michael VICKERS
Structure and Conflict in Nigeria 1960-66 (London:
Heinemann, 1973)   248 pp.
Bibliography.

Authors argue that events of period centering around
1964-5 election of new federal legislature constituted
prolonged crisis of political system in Nigeria; introduce conceptual models based on political theory to
assist in explanations.

11. Senegal

FOUGEYROLLAS, Pierre
   Ou Va le Senegal? (IFAN, Dakar; Paris: Editions Anthropos, 1970)   274 pp.

   Written by Frenchman living in Senegal. Discusses aspirations of Senegalese people vis-a-vis economic and political development and need to free itself from vestiges of colonialism/imperialism and establish own African identity. Socio-political analysis based on empirical study from interviews and questionnaires.

GAUTRON, Jean-Claude
   L'Administration Senegalaise (Encyclopedie Administrative; Paris: Editions Berger-Levrault, 1971)   94 pp.
   Bibliography.

   Useful description of structure and functions of Senegalese administration; Senegal may be considered unique case in African administration because of French and Islam influences combined.

GONIDEC, P.F.
   La Republique du Senegal (Encyclopedie Politique et Constitutionnelle; Paris: Editions Berger-Levrault, 1968) 62 pp.
   Bibliography.

   Introduction to socio-political setting, political/constitutional evolution and current regime in Senegal; includes text of constitution.

LAVROFF, D.G.
   La Republique du Senegal (Paris: Librairie Generale de Droit et de Jurisprudence, 1966)   257 pp.
   Bibliography.

   Studies nature of Senegalese society, political institutions as set down in constitution and political forces/political parties and their role in functioning of political institutions. Puts political system in perspective of society as whole.

SCHUMACHER, Edward J.
   Politics, Bureaucracy and Rural Development in Senegal (Berkeley: University of California Press, 1973) 320 pp.

   Examines how leadership of Senegal has responded to rural development during first decade of independence.

12. Sierra Leone

KILSON, Martin
  Political Change in a West African State: a study of the
  modernization process in Sierra Leone   (Cambridge, Mass.:
  Harvard University Press, 1966)   301 pp.
  Bibliography.

  In historical context and in terms of comparative analysis of African political change, studies political
  change and modernization process that produced indigenous political elite and studies governmental institutions
  now controlled by that elite.

13. Togo

CORNEVIN, Robert
  Le Togo   (Paris: Presses Universitaires de France, 1973)
  128 pp.
  Bibliography.

  Covers socio-political setting, precolonial period, German and then French colony, and introduces independent
  Togo.   Contains some useful maps and statistics but is
  very much an introductory study.

14. Upper Volta

LIPPENS, Philippe
  La Republique de Haute-Volta   (Encyclopedie Politique et
  Constitutionnelle, Institut International d'Administra-
  tion Publique;   Paris: Editions Bergers- Levrault, 1972)
  63 pp.
  Bibliography.

  Studies society and political evolution; examines different political forces and notably, new constitution.

SKINNER, Elliott P.
  The Mossi of the Upper Volta: the political development
  of a Sudanese people   (Stanford, Calif.: Stanford University Press, 1964)
  Bibliography.

  Political/anthropological analysis of society that has
  maintained most of traditional structures of government
  of medieval kingdoms.

C. POLITICAL PARTIES, INTEREST GROUPS AND IDEOLOGIES

CROWDER, Michael, and Obaro IKIMA, eds.
West African Chiefs: their changing status under colonial
rule and independence (New York: African Publishing
Corporation, 1970; Ife Ife, Nigeria: University of Ife
Press, 1970) 453 pp.
Bibliography.

Papers are from seminar held by Institute of African
Studies at University of Ife in December 1968. Consider
nature of indirect rule in colonial period and differences between French and British administrations in colonial period. Try to better understand nature of institution of chieftaincy.

MAHIOU, Ahmed
L'Avenement du Parti Unique en Afrique Noire: l'exper-
ience des etats d'expression francaise (Paris: Librair-
ie Generale de Droit et de Jurisprudence, R. Pichon et
R. Durand-Auzias, 1969) 421 pp.
Bibliography.

Studies mechanism of evolution of single party, reasons
and factors in evolution of single party, and results of
that evolution (structure and ideology).

Politique et Ideologie en Afrique (Presence Africaine, No. 63,
2nd quarter (1967), Paris) pp. 10-119.

Selected articles focusing on problems and development
of African political institutions and various ideologies
such as Pan-Africanism, Negritude, etc.

SCHACHTER-MORGENTHAU, Ruth
Political Parties in French-speaking West Africa (Oxford:
Clarendon Press, 1964) 445 pp.
Bibliography.

Book referred to in many more recent books; her approach
of using country studies has been copied by many after
her. Chapters separately on Ivory Coast, Guinea, Mali,
Senegal. Approach is from specific to general; also
treats historical development of political parties in
context of French colonial period and professes to general party theory conclusions. Appendices include French
constitutions and information concerning African political leaders.

WILSON, Henry S.
 Origins of West African Nationalism (London: Macmillan,
 1969) 391 pp.
 Bibliography.

 Author uses series of documents to explore origins of
 concepts of nationhood and independence in English-
 speaking West Africa; probes ideology and attitudes in
 depth.

ZOLBERG, Aristide R.
 Creating Political Order: the party-states of West Africa
 (Chicago: Rand McNally, 1966)   168 pp.

 Studies relate to five countries: Ivory Coast, Mali,
 Ghana, Senegal, Guinea. Discusses emergence of dominant
 party systems, ideology on which they are based, obstacles to their authority, and instruments of their rule.
 All of this put in context of theoretical framework of
 political science and in perspective of study of new
 African states.

1. Benin (Dahomey)

HAZOUME, Guy Landry
 Ideologies Tribalistes et Nation en Afrique: le cas
 dahomeen (Paris: Presence Africaine, 1972)   230 pp.
 Bibliography.

 Takes approach of political anthropology to discuss
 phenomenon of tribalist ideology in Benin; considers
 social and political functions of those ideologies and
 their relation to the concept of nation (sees tribalism
 as source of conflict and oppression, and recourse in
 revolution).

2. Cameroon

BETI, Mongo
 Main Basse sur le Cameroun: autopsie d'une decolonisation
 (Paris: Francois Maspero, 1972)   217 pp.

 Anti-imperialist approach regarding French involvement
 in Cameroon. In particular, recounts events leading up
 to and including trial in Yaounde (1970-71); stresses
 apathy demonstrated by international community regarding
 death sentences imposed on Ernest Ouandie, etc.

4. Ghana

DAMACHI, U.G.
The Role of the Trade Unions in the Development Process:
with a case study of Ghana   (New York: Praeger, 1974)
175 pp.
Bibliography.

Analyzes labour movement in Ghana under phases of two-
party government, one-party government, and under military regime, and then makes inter-period comparison.
Studies trade unions in relation to broader political
system, especially government itself.

6. Ivory Coast

ZOLBERG, Aristide R.
One-Party Government in the Ivory Coast   (Princeton, N.J.:
Princeton University Press, 1964)   374 pp.
Bibliography.

In traditional approach to development of political parties, describes emergence of single-party system despite
existence of strong ethnic rivalries and discusses structures of government used to create cohesive nation-state.
Argues that it may not be appropriate in African context
to associate multi-party state with democracy and one-
party state with totalitarianism.

8. Mali

SNYDER, Frank Gregory
One-Party Government in Mali   (New Haven: Yale University
Press, 1965)   178 pp.
Bibliography.

Traces origins and development of Union-Soudanaise-RDA,
and relates these aspects to its behaviour in post-independence Mali, e.g., how pre-independence nationalist
party adapts to post-independence changes and challenges.
Appendices include several relevant political documents.

10. Nigeria

ANANABA, Wogu
The Trade Union Movement in Nigeria   (London: C. Hurst
& Co., 1969)   336 pp.

History of movement from 1912 to 1966: emphasizes multi-
plicity and factionalism of unions and related problems.
Suggests means of reconstructing movement so as to in-
crease bargaining power.   Appendices include documents.

CERVENKA, Zdenek
   The Nigerian War: 1967-70 (Frankfurt-am-Main: Bernard
   & Graefe Verlag fur Wehrwesen, 1971)   459 pp.
   Bibliography (72 pp.).

   Account begins with events of 15 January 1966; discusses
   military rule of General Ironsi and Lt. Colonel Gowon,
   causes of secession of Biafra and of outbreak of war.
   Main part of book concerns military operations, arms and
   strategy employed, and factors which influenced course of
   war. Documents are directly relevant to chapters.

COHEN, Abner
   Custom and Politics in Urban Africa (London: Routledge
   & Kegan Paul, 1969)   252 pp.

   Study of Hausa migrants in Yoruba towns. Considers role
   of custom in politics in some contemporary urban settings
   in Africa: how an ethnic group manipulates some values,
   norms, beliefs, symbols and ceremonials from its traditional culture in order to develop formal political organization which it uses as weapon in its struggle for
   power with other groups.

DUDLEY, B.J.
   Parties and Politics in Northern Nigeria (London: Frank
   Cass, 1968)   352 pp.
   Bibliography.

   Discusses evolution of politics in Northern Nigeria and
   how it relates to Nigerian federalism; explains traditional socio-political organization, emergence of political parties, treating each major party separately and
   showing how it relates to grass roots. Appendices include documents concerning political parties.

KIRK-GREEN, A.H.M.
   Crisis and Conflict in Nigeria: a documentary sourcebook
   1966-1969 (London: Oxford University Press, 1971)
   987 pp. Two volumes.
   Bibliography.

   Documentation includes only actual declarations of con-
   tending political groups and their propaganda machinery,
   recorded in their own words and whenever possible at
   the very time. Includes very little second-hand or
   third-party data, but occasionally includes local evaluation of a situation or event. Covers period of Nigerian civil war (January 1966 - January 1970).

LUCKHAM, Robin
The Nigerian Military: a sociological analysis of author-
ity and revolt 1960-67 (Cambridge: Cambridge University
Press, 1971)   376 pp.

Socio-political approach; argues that military institutions even in new states which faced fundamental threat
to their authority and existence, as in Nigeria, can be
seen to have structure, pattern and vitality of their
own. Utilizes organization model of professional military; studies problems of institutional transfer; concerned with approaches/models of civil-military relations.

SKLAR, Richard L.
Nigerian Political Parties: power in an emergent African
nation (Princeton, N.J.: Princeton University Press,
1963)   578 pp.
Bibliography.

Important study of development of Nigerian party system
during last decade of British colonial rule. In particular, makes series of case studies in power and conflict
relating to specific parties; analyzes relation between
party structure and social structure.

SMOCK, Audrey C.
Ibo Politics: the role of ethnic unions in Eastern Nigeria
(Cambridge, Mass.: Harvard University Press, 1971) 274 pp.
Bibliography.

Study concentrates on political systems of two Ibo communities in Eastern Nigeria: Abiriba and Mbaise. Emphasis
on role that ethnic unions played in these micropolitical
systems and their effect on local political development.
Ethnic union: combines modern structure and functions of
voluntary association with an ascriptive membership base.

SMOCK, David R.
Conflict and Control in an African Trade Union: a study
of the Nigerian Coal Miners' Union (Stanford, Calif.:
Hoover Institution Press, 1969)   170 pp.
Bibliography.

Detailed analysis of African trade union, focussed on
understanding reasons for highly centralizes and autocratic leadership of union and for extensive leadership
disputes and internal conflict.

11. Senegal

BEHRMAN, Lucy
Muslim Brotherhoods and Politics in Senegal (Cambridge,
Mass.: Harvard University Press, 1970)   224 pp.

Discusses relationship between Senghor's government and
Muslim brotherhoods, i.e. serves as link between government and peasantry, perhaps as substitute for real political participation. Discusses what sort of effect this
relationship might have on modernization process in long
run -- brotherhoods represent a traditional and conservative element in Senegalese society.

CRUISE O'BRIEN, Donal B.
The Mourides of Senegal: the political and economic or-
ganization of an Islamic brotherhood (Oxford: Clarendon
Press, 1971)   321 pp.
Bibliography.

Historical introduction describes Mourides from origins
(c. 1886-1945). Sociological account of structure and
evolution of religious authority and relations surrounding economic production (hierarchy, political dominance,
submission, associations) and discusses forces working
to change brotherhood.

CRUISE O'BRIEN, Donal B.
Saints and Politicians: essays in the organization of a
Senegalese peasant society (London: Cambridge Universit
Press, 1975)   213 pp.
Bibliography.

Discusses political theme concerning organizational response of Wolof people to colonial rule and argues that
this response is reproduced in relations between formal
state apparatus and rural mass of Wolof; author is especially interested in role of various intermediaries.

CRUISE O'BRIEN, Rita
White Society in Black Africa: the French in Senegal
(London: Faber & Faber, 1972)   320 pp.
Bibliography.

Looks at interaction of white minority with African Senegalese people against background of structures and
attitudes from former colonial period in order to see
what sort of independence from France has actually been
achieved -- French in Senegal still play crucial role in
government and society.

ZUCCARELLI, Francois
   Un Parti Politique Africain: l'Union Progressiste Senegalaise (Paris: Librairie Generale de Droit et de Jurisprudence, R. Pichon et R. Durand-Auzias, 1970)   401 pp.
   Bibliography.

   Studies origins of political parties in Senegal between
   1875-1969, then considers case of dominant party in Senegal (UPS): its organization, function, role within political system, its relation to African socialism. Annexes
   provide relevant documentation.

D. BIOGRAPHIES, MEMOIRS, SPEECHES, WRITINGS
BY POLITICAL LEADERS

2. Cameroon

WOUNGLY-MASSAGA
   L'Afrique Bloquee: l'example du Kamerun -- problemes de
   la lutte populaire apres l'assassinat d'Ernest Ouandie
   (Geneva: Centre d'information sur les mouvements de liberation, 1974)   255 pp.

   Written by leader of l'Union des Populations du Cameroun
   (UPC). Discusses question of one-party state particularly in circumstances of complex ethnic diversity and heritage of two colonial powers; analyzes power struggle,
   goals and tactics of UPC working towards democratic,
   representative regime.

4. Ghana

ARMAH, Kwesi
   Ghana: Nkrumah's Legacy (London: Rex Collings, 1974)
   185 pp.
   Bibliography.

   Written by member of Nkrumah's government (minister of
   trade): 'Partly a reflection of my experiences, partly
   an attempt to describe Ghana's struggle for political
   and economic independence, and partly an assessment of
   the legacy of Kwame Nkrumah'. Also evaluates administration of National Liberation Council which took over from
   Nkrumah and Second Republic under Dr. Busia's Progress
   Party: argues that they have not solved problems left by
   Nkrumah but have made some worse; in particular, argues
   that Ghana's role in African politics as whole has de-
   clined and with it, Ghana's prestige.

BRETTON, Henry L.
The Rise and Fall of Kwame Nkrumah   (London: Pall Mall
Press, 1967)   232 pp.
Bibliography.

Besides its concern with role and function of one political personality, study also emphasizes Nkrumah's political machine, nature and role of sole political party
and of ideology, and effects of personal rule on government and administration.

BUSIA, K.A.
Africa in Search of Democracy   (London: Routledge &
Kegan Paul, 1967)   189 pp.
Bibliography.

Discusses two views of democracy: Marxist-Leninist and
Western, in African context and argues that present task
in Africa is to do away with repressive government; relates democracy to religious and tribal heritage and
tries to assess whether African nations have been able
to incorporate democratic principles into its new socio-
political framework. Busia became leader of Ghana after
coup that overthrew Nkrumah.

BUSIA, K.A.
The Challenge of Africa   (New York: Praeger, 1962; London: Pall Mall Press, 1962)   150 pp.

Essay concerns four aspects of African nationalism which
Busia describes as challenge of culture, challenge of
colonial experience, challenge of common humanity and
morality, and challenge of responsible emancipation.

DAVIDSON, Basil
Black Star: a view of the life and times of Kwame Nkrumah
(London: Allen Lane, 1973)   225 pp.

This biography emphasizes contradictions in Nkrumah's
character which led to both strengths and weaknesses in
his regime. Most recent study. Argues that Nkrumah's
persistent inability to correct bureaucratic degeneration
of CPP is main lesson of his fall from power; contends
that CPP was unable to mobilize masses partly because
revolutionary situation did not exist in Ghana.

IKOKU, Samuel G.
Le Ghana de Nkrumah   (Paris: Francois Maspero, 1971)
234 pp.

Covers period 1957-66. Analysis of Nkrumah's regime

which deals, in particular, with question of which path
of development did Nkrumah choose to follow? What sort
of revolution did he foresee for Ghana and how was his
policy manifested in reality? Author analyzes carefully
CPP and its organization, ideologies, etc. and considers
causes of 'counter-revolution'.

NKRUMAH, Kwame
The Autobiography of Kwame Nkrumah (Edinburgh: Thomas
Nelson & Sons, Ltd., 1957)   310 pp.

Written just prior to Ghana's independence, provides
insights into Nkrumah's goals and intellectual/political
development. Also describes formation of CPP and struggle
for independence - from leader's point of view.

NKRUMAH, Kwame
I Speak of Freedom (London: Heinemann, 1961)   291 pp.

Nkrumah describes his role in independence struggle in
Ghana and in early post-independence years. Uses many
excerpts from speeches, etc. Emphasizes desire for African unity which he sees as necessary for development;
also demonstrates his aim that Ghana should play leading
role in world and African affairs.

OMARI, T. Peter
Kwame Nkrumah: the anatomy of an African dictatorship
(London: C. Hurst & Co., 1970)   229 pp.
Bibliography.

Critical analysis of Nkrumah's government; cites one of
his chief weaknesses as being his tendency to rely on
morally weak opportunists to promote his policies at
home and abroad, but at same time criticizes Nkrumah's
opponents for not acting in strong enough manner to curb
Nkrumah's faults in earlier stages of his rule. Final
chapter analyzes prospects for Ghana after 1966 coup.

Hommage a Kwame Nkrumah (Presence Africaine, No. 85 (1973),
Paris) 186 pp.

Includes articles both in French and English by such
people as Amilcar Cabral, S.S. Adotevi, J. Berque, Samuel G. Ikoku, Yves Benot, Jean Suret-Canale, Thomas
Hodgkin, etc. Articles emphasize Nkrumah's philosophy/
ideology and his personal impact on decolonization process in Africa.

5. Guinea

TOURE, Ahmed Sekou
>   L'Afrique et la Revolution   (Paris: Presence Africaine,
>   n.d.)   398 pp.

Exposition of history and doctrine of Parti Democratique
de Guinee (PDG), written by its head for the use of party
cadres; therefore, written in form of questions and
answers.

TOURE, Ahmed Sekou
>   L'Experience Guineenne et l'Unite Africaine   (Paris:
>   Presence Africaine, 1961)   436 pp.

Chronology of nationalist movement in Guinea, role
played by Toure, and implications for development of
rest of Africa.

10. Nigeria

AWOLOWO, Chief Obafemi
>   Awo: the autobiography of Chief Obafemi Awolowo   (Cam-
>   bridge: Cambridge University Press, 1960)   316 pp.

Autobiography of one of major architects of Nigerian
nationalism.

AWOLOWO, Chief Obafemi
>   The People's Republic   (Ibadan: Oxford University Press,
>   1968)   356 pp.

Written while author served as federal commissioner of
finance. Part I discusses period of British rule in
Nigeria. Part II is exposition of 'political, economic
and social principles which are of universal application
and validity': meant to provide rationale for clean
break with British administration heritage and need for
acceptance of 'blueprint' proposed in Part III. Consists
of author's proposals for federal system of government/
administration. Provides specific outline of entire system - a scholarly and well-thought-out discussion.

OJUKWU, C. Odumegwu
>   Biafra: Volume I. Selected Speeches   (390 pp.)
>   Volume II. Random Thoughts   (226 pp.)
>   (New York: Perennial Library, Harper & Row, 1969)

Ojukwu was leader of Biafra in Nigerian civil war. Argues that in order to be truly independent, African nations require African ideology which is of equal dynam-
ism to those imposed by colonialists.

11. Senegal

MARKOVITZ, Irving Leonard
  Leopold Sedar Senghor and the Politics of Negritude
  (London: Heinemann, 1969)   300 pp.
  Bibliography.

  Critical study of relation between Senghor's ideology
  and his political regime, and also relevance of his
  theories and values to socio-political scene in Senegal.

MILCENT, Ernest, and Monique SORDET
  Leopold Sedar Senghor et la Naissance de l'Afrique
  Moderne (Paris: Editions Seghers, 1969)   271 pp.
  Bibliography.

  Takes rather journalistic approach but provides interesting discussion of Senghor's career and his ideas.

ROUS, Jean
  Leopold Sedar Senghor: la vie d'un president de l'Afrique nouvelle (Paris: Editions John Didier, 1967)
  163 pp.

  Biography of Senghor written by Frenchman who was
  Senghor's political adviser and friend; account is therefore biased in his favour. Gives introduction to various facets of Senghor's life and, in particular, as
  president of Senegal.

12. Sierra Leone

COLLIER, Gershon
  Sierra Leone: experiment in democracy in an African nation
  (New York: New York University Press, 1970)   143 pp.

  Author was barrister, ambassador, minister, chief justice and scholar in Sierra Leone; was supporter of
  Prime Minister Albert Margai. Writes as 'participant
  observer' in discussing political evolution of Sierra
  Leone. Provides interesting insights into political
  life in post-independence period, problems of establishing democracy, etc.

E. EXTERNAL RELATIONS

FOLTZ, William J.
From French West Africa to the Mali Federation   (New
Haven: Yale University Press, 1965)   235 pp.

Book tries to answer two questions: why was Mali Federation formed? why did it fail? In more general terms,
tries to study problems facing political unions (inter-
state) in developing countries and to see how those problems and conditions compare with those existing for
political unions in Western Europe and North America.
Also considers effects of colonial heritage on potential
for political union.

THOMPSON, Virginia
West Africa's Council of the Entente   (Ithaca, N.Y.:
Cornell University Press, 1972)   313 pp.
Bibliography.

Studies origin and nature of Council of the Entente
(Niger, Dahomey, Upper Volta, Togo, Ivory Coast). Particularly concerned with leadership of Houphouet-Boigny of
Ivory Coast and with political events in each of member
countries.

WELCH, Claude E., Jr.
Dream of Unity: Pan-Africanism and political unification
in West Africa   (Ithaca, N.Y.: Cornell University Press,
1966)   396 pp.
Bibliography.

Examines four attempts by African states to achieve
closer political relations at time of independence,
during transfer of power from colonial administration to
African government. Cases: Togoland, Cameroun, Senegambia,
Ghana/Guinea/Mali. Argues that as countries develop
their individual governments and economies, pressures
towards unification with other states become less immed-
iate.

4. Ghana

THOMPSON, W. Scott
Ghana's Foreign Policy 1957-66   (Princeton, N.J.: Princeton University Press, 1969)   462 pp.

Discusses Ghana as example of new state which developed
considerable diplomatic and military instruments and became more realistic about nature of international system.
Studies relation between domestic and foreign policies.

NORTH AFRICA

A. POLITICAL HISTORY

ABUN-NASR, Jamil M.
A History of the Maghrib (Cambridge: Cambridge University Press, 1971) 416 pp.
Bibliography.

General history of north-west Africa (Algeria, Libya, Morocco, Tunisia).

BERQUE, Jacques
French North Africa: the Maghrib between two World Wars (London: Faber & Faber, 1967)

Originally published in French (Paris: Editions du Seuil, 1962). Covers period 1918-39: sensitive collection of studies largely concerning defeat of French colonial system; characterizes many aspects of life in Maghrib at that time.

GORDON, David C.
North Africa's French Legacy 1954-62 (for Centre for Middle Eastern Studies; Cambridge, Mass.: Harvard University Press, 1962) 121 pp.
Bibliography.

Considers nature of Westernized elites of Tunisia, Morocco, Algeria; asks whether French-educated elite can integrate Arab legacy with French colonial heritage and avoid sort of confrontation foreseen by Frantz Fanon; compares situation in each of three countries.

JULIEN, Charles-Andre
L'Afrique du Nord en Marche: nationalismes musulmans et souverainete francaise (Paris: Julliard, 1972) 439 pp.
Bibliography (extensive).

History of nationalist movement and French rule in Tunisia, Morocco and Algeria, based on author's personal experience and acquaintance with many of participants.

JULIEN, Charles-Andre
Histoire de l'Afrique du Nord de la Conquete Arabe a
1830 (Paris: Payot, 1964)   2 Volumes.
Bibliography (extensive).

Translated to English; published London, 1970. Standard
political history of Tunisia, Algeria and Morocco.

TOURNEAU, Roger le
Evolution Politique de l'Afrique du Nord Musulmane 1920-
1961 (Paris: Librairie Armand Colin, 1962)   503 pp.
Bibliography.

Treats political evolution of Tunisia, Morocco and Algeria after presenting sketch of society in region; for
Tunisia and Morocco includes discussion of period following independence.

1. Algeria

AGERON, Charles-Robert
Histoire de l'Algerie Contemporaine 1830-1964 (Paris:
Presses Universitaires de France, 1964)

Short history which draws on author's extensive research.

AGERON, Charles-Robert
Politiques Coloniales au Maghreb (Paris: Presses Universitaires de France, 1972)   288 pp.

Series of historical essays on French policy in Algeria
and response of early Algerian nationalists.

ARON, Raymond
L'Algerie et la Republique (Paris: 1958)

Sequel to author's La Tragedie Algerienne.

ARON, Raymond
La Tragedie Algerienne (Paris: Plon, 1957)   76 pp.

Political essay which stresses force of Algerian nationalism and necessity for political solution to Algerian
'impasse'.

ARON, Robert, ed.
Les Origines de la Guerre d'Algerie (Paris: 1962)

Somewhat uneven collection of essays prepared under impact of Algerian war.

BEHR, Edward
   The Algerian Problem   (London: Penguin Books, 1961)
   256 pp.

   Journalist's account of origins of war of independence,
   the war and its importance for French politics. Balanced
   and informative.

BENNABI, Malek
   Memoires d'un Temoin du Siecle   (Algiers: 1965)

   Rare insight into political developments and social
   change in Algeria in early twentieth century.

BURON, Robert
   Carnets Politiques de la Guerre d'Algerie   (Paris: Plon,
   1965)   267 pp.

   Diary of participant in Evian negotiations, written from
   first day of Algerian war to its conclusion.

CLARK, Michael K.
   Algeria in Turmoil   (London: Thames & Hudson, 1960)
   452 pp.

   Survey which begins with cursory historical background.
   Second and major part covers period from outbreak of war
   of independence to de Gaulle's access to power. Argues
   urgent need for integration of Algeria into France. Outdated in some respects but contains observations of
   permanent interest.

COURRIERE, Yves
   La Guerre d'Algerie   (Paris: Fayard, 1968-72) 5 Vols.

   Journalist's history which provides best-informed account
   of Algerian war. Invaluable for narrative; does not
   attempt extended analysis.
   Vol. I: Les fils de la Toussaint (1968) - the origins of
   the insurrection and opening of conflict.
   Vol. II: Le temps des leopards (1969) - years 1955-7
   including Battle of Algiers.
   Vol. III: L'heure des colonels (1970) - insurrection of
   13 May 1958 and setting up of GPRA.
   Vol. IV: Les feux du desespoir (1971) - conclusion of
   war; negotiations leading to Evian agreement; OAS.

GORDON, David C.
The Passing of French Algeria   (London: Oxford University
Press, 1966)   246 pp.
Bibliography.

Brief historical introduction on nineteenth century
Algeria and the 'abandoned chance' of Blum's government.
Major part of book a discussion of 'men' and 'ideas' of
Algerian nationalism.

JULIEN, Charles-Andre
Histoire de l'Algerie Contemporaine   (Paris: 1964)
Bibliography (extensive).

Covers period 1830-1870; political and general history
which surveys political development and social change
under French rule.   Illustrated.

KESSEL, Patrick, and Giovanni PIRELLI, eds.
Le Peuple Algerien et la Guerre   (Paris: Francois Maspero,
1962)   716 pp.

Documentary collection of letters and comments by Algerians who experienced war of independence in Algeria, in
France and in prison.

LACOSTE, Yves, Andre NOUSCHI, and Andre PRENANT
L'Algerie Passe et Present   (Paris: 1960)

Collection of essays published during war of independence
to present an impartial account to French public.   Provides valuable surveys of colonization, property and
land questions as well as growth of nationalism.

LUCAS, Philippe, and Jean-Claude VATIN
L'Algerie des Anthropologues   (Paris: 1975)

Analyzes perceptions of Algeria found in and propagated
by Frenchscholarly writing, particularly historical
accounts.

O'BALLANCE, Edgar
The Algerian Insurrection 1954-62   (London: Faber &
Faber, 1967)   229 pp.

Straightforward account of the war which has since been
overtaken by more recent knowledge.

PAILLAT, Claude
Les Dossiers Secrets de l'Algerie   (Paris: 1962)   2 Vols.

Episodic account of Algerian war based on sources which
are often not identified.

PICKLES, Dorothy
  Algeria and France: from colonialism to co-operation
  (London: 1963)

  Surveys impact of Algerian question and war of independence on French politics.

VATIN, Jean-Claude
  L'Algerie Politique: histoire et societe   (Paris: Armand
  Colin, 1974)

  History of Algeria mainly since French conquest, and
  sensitive therefore to gaps in existing knowledge and
  limitations of accepted ideas.

2. Libya

EVANS-PRITCHARD, E.E.
  The Sanusi of Cyrenaica   (Oxford: Clarendon Press, 1949)
  240 pp.
  Bibliography.

  History (1837-1942) of development of Sanusiya Order
  among Bedouin tribes; emphasizes political and economic
  organization of Sanusiya because that differentiates it
  from most other Islamic orders; describes Italo-Sanusi
  relations at length.

PELT, Adrian
  Libyan Independence and the United Nations   (New Haven:
  Yale University Press, 1970)   1016 pp.

  Detailed study of diplomacy leading to independence by
  the responsible UN official.

WRIGHT, John
  Libya (London: Benn, 1969)   280 pp.
  Bibliography.

  Lively historical survey from earliest times until last
  year of old regime. Valuable detailed information on
  politics since World War II.

3. Mauritania

ABUN-NASR, Jamil M.
  The Tijanniya (Oxford: Oxford University Press, 1965)

  Standard account of one of most important religious
  orders in Mauritania.

STEWART, C.G., and E.K. STEWART
Islam and Social Order in Mauritania (Oxford: Clarendon Press, 1973)

Largely historical account of Shaikh Sidiyya and his economic and political influence in nineteenth century.

4. Morocco

BARBOUR, Nevill
Morocco (London: Thames & Hudson, 1965)   239 pp.

Well balanced historical survey leading to discussion of politics, economy and society at time of writing.

BERNARD, Stephane
The Franco-Moroccan Conflict 1943-56 (New Haven: Yale University Press, 1968)   680 pp.

Also in French, 3 Vols., published by Editions de l'Institut de Sociologie de l'Universite Libre de Bruxelles, 1963. Detailed interpretative analysis.

BIDWELL, Robin
Morocco Under Colonial Rule: French administration of tribal areas 1912-56 (London: Frank Cass, 1973) 346 pp.

Valuable account of French protectorate policy; role of Lyautey; economic and land questions; policies towards great caids; effect on tribes.

BLEUCHOT, Hene
Les Liberaux Francais au Maroc 1947-55 (Provence: Editions de l'Universite de Provence, 1973) 282 pp. Bibliography.

Defines, identifies and analyzes role of liberals amongst French community and their part in movement towards independence. Documentary appendix.

GALLISOT, Rene
Le Patronat Europeen au Maroc 1931-42 (Rabat: Editions Techniques Nord-Africains, 1964) 283 pp.

Account of growth of French society under protectorate which provides useful background to political development.

JULY, Pierre
Une Republique pour un Roi (Paris: Fayard, 1974) 285 pp.

Personal account of relations between France and Moroccan nationalist movement from 1954 to independence, with valuable insights on conference of Aix-les-Bains.

MIEGE, Jean-Louis
   Le Maroc et l'Europe 1830-94 (Paris: 1962) 4 Vols.

   Magistral survey which covers political, consular and
   commercial relationships. Vol. I is entirely devoted
   to sources and bibliography.

MONTAGNE, Robert
   Les Berberes et le Makhzen dans le Sud du Maroc (Paris:
   Felix Alcan, 1930) 426 pp.

   Classic account of history and political structure of
   Berbers of Sons province.

MONTAGNE, Robert
   Revolution au Maroc (Paris: Editions France-Empire,
   1951) 415 pp.

   Political survey designed to 'clarify the ideas of French-
   men' during crisis of protectorate; urges 'acceleration
   of the social and political development of the Moroccan
   people'; also argues that ideas of radical Moroccans are
   unlikely to be realizes unless they understand nature of
   traditional Moroccan society.

SCHAM, Alan
   Lyautey in Morocco (Berkeley: University of California
   Press, 1970) 273 pp.

   Critical account of Lyautey's rule and its impact on
   Moroccan government and society.

SPILLMAN, Georges
   Du Protectorat a l'Independance: Maroc 1912-55 (Paris:
   Plon, 1967) 245 pp.

   Episodic account of relations between France and Morocco
   based on personal memoirs.

TERRASSE, H.
   Histoire du Maroc (Casablanca: 1950) 2 Vols.

   Standard history, from earliest times to establishment
   of French protectorate.

WOOLMAN, David
   Rebels in the Rif: Abd El Krim and the Rif Rebellion
   (London: Oxford University Press, 1969; Stanford, Calif.:
   Stanford University Press, 1969) 256 pp.

   Account of revolt of Abd El Krim based on recent research.

5. Tunisia

BASSET, A. et al.
  Initiation a la Tunisie (Paris: 1950)

  General survey which provides useful perspectives on
  period preceding independence.

BROWN, Leon Carl
  The Surest Path: a translation of the introduction to the
  'Surest Path to Knowledge Concerning the Condition of
  Countries', by Khayr al-Din al-Tunisi (Cambridge, Mass.:
  Harvard University Press, 1967)

  Translation, with introduction, of the work of political
  philosophy written by Tunisia's outstanding nineteenth
  century reformer.

Centre de Documentation Nationale
  Histoire du Mouvement National (Tunis: various dates)

  Official publication providing an account of the nationalist movement, focusing particularly on Bourguiba and
  the Med Deston.

GANIAGE, Jean
  Les Origines du Protectorat Francais en Tunisie (Paris:
  1959)

  Magistral work on its subject which provides historical
  insight into Tunisia as well as an account of European
  politics.

KING, Dwight L.
  Tunisia from Protectorate to Republic (Bloomington, Ind.:
  Indiana University Press, 1967)   272 pp.

  Brief, sometimes superficial account of protectorate and
  movement to independence.

TAALBI, Shaikh
  La Tunisie Martyre (Paris: 1920) Published anonymously.

  Tract which expounds author's view of his country's
  heritage under pressure of French domination and which
  provided political philosophy of Deston party.

B. POLITICAL SYSTEMS, GOVERNMENT

AMIN, Samir
The Maghreb in the Modern World   (London: Penguin, 1970)
256 pp.

French edition, Le Maghreb Moderne (Paris: 1970).
General survey of French colonization, establishment of
independent states of Algeria, Tunisia, Morocco, and
review of their social and economic characteristics.
Author's view is that 'the analysis of the economic consequences of colonial exploitation is fundamental to an
understanding of the region'. In spite of title, there
is little detailed reference to international position
of Maghreb. Borrows from author's L'Economie du Maghreb
(Paris: Editions de Minuit, 1966).

BROWN, L.C., ed.
State and Society in Independent North Africa   (Washington, D.C.: The Middle East Institute, 1966)   332 pp.

Invaluable collection of essays on political parties,
foreign policy, religion, culture and economy. Authors
include Zartman, Gallagher, Berque, Issawi, Monroe.

Centre de Recherches et Etudes sur les Societes Mediterraneennes
Introduction a l'Afrique du Nord Contemporaine   (Paris:
Centre National de la Recherche Scientifique, 1975)
449 pp.
Bibliography.

Collection of articles by eighteen different authors on
economy, politics and society of Algeria, Tunisia,
Morocco; cover wide range of topics without being welded
into coherent whole. Chronology.

KNAPP, Wilfrid
North West Africa: a political and economic survey
(London: Oxford University Press, 1976)   427 pp.

Third edition of Neville Barbour.'s Survey of North West
Africa (London: Oxford University Press, 1959), com-
pletely rewritten except for historical passages.
Chapter by Robert Mabro on economy of Libya and by Robin
Ostle on literature (French and Arab) in North West Africa.
Covers Algeria, Libya, Mauritania, Morocco and Tunisia.

MOORE, Clement Henry
  Politics in North Africa   (Boston: Little Brown, 1970)
  360 pp.

  Volume in Little Brown series designed to provide introduction to politics through common functionalist approach.
  Covers Algeria, Morocco, Tunisia.

ZARTMAN, I. William
  Government and Politics in Northern Africa   (London:
  Methuen, 1964)   205 pp.

  Introduction on 'democracy and independence' precedes
  survey of politics of Morocco, Algeria, Tunisia, Libya,
  United Arab Republic, Sudan, Ethiopia, Somalia. Of limited value given its brevity and date of publication.

1. Algeria

AGERON, Charles Robert
  Les Algeriens Musulmans et la France   (Paris: Presses
  Universitaires de France, 1968)   2 Vols.   1298 pp.

  Magistral work which provides account of politics, administration, property, education, religion, etc. Extensive
  bibliography.

BOURDIEU, Pierre
  The Algerians   (Boston: 1962)

  Translation of Sociologie de l'Algerie   (Paris: 1958).
  Basic sociological/anthropological study.

CHALIAND, Gerard
  L'Algerie: est-elle socialiste?   (Paris: Francois Maspero,
  1964)   168 pp.

  To which author gives a qualified negative answer.

CHALIAND, Gerard, and Juliette MINCES
  L'Algerie Independante   (Paris: Francois Maspero, 1972)
  173 pp.

  Observations of two intellectuals visiting Algeria at
  end of first decade of independence; many perceptive
  insights which spring from disappointed hopes.

HUMBARACI, Arslan
  Algeria: a revolution that failed   (London: Pall Mall
  Press, 1966)   271 pp.

  Following introductory chapters on historical background
  and war of independence, major part is concerned with

period of Ben Bella's rule. In journalistic and tenden-
tious account, author examines failure to achieve 'socialist revolution'.

MERGHOUB, Baelhadj
  Le Developpement Politique en Algerie (Paris: Armand
  Colin, 1972) 175 pp.

  Monograph on region of the Mzab in southern Algeria: its
  history and integration into Algerian political system,
  including development of local government.

OTTAWAY, David and Marina
  Algeria: the politics of a socialist revolution (Berke-
  ley/Los Angeles: University of California Press, 1970)
  322 pp.
  Bibliography.

  Perceptive account by journalists of political developments from independence to aftermath of Boumediene coup
  (1965). Useful biographies of leading politicians.

REMILI, Abderrahmane
  Les Institutions Administratives Algeriennes (Algiers:
  1968)

  Comprehensive account of formal structure of Algerian
  state.

VIRATELLE, Gerard
  L'Algerie Algerienne (Paris: Editions Ouvrieres, 1970)
  309 pp.

  Political and economic survey of first eight years of
  independence based on author's observations as Le Monde
  correspondent.

2. Libya

FIRST, Ruth
  Libya: the elusive revolution (London: Penguin, 1974)
  294 pp.

  Useful study of politics and ideology of Qaddafi's Libya,
  and review of early years of economic development.

KHADDURI, Majid
  Modern Libya: a study in political development (Baltimore: Johns Hopkins University Press, 1963) 404 pp.

  Provides brief historical introduction; discusses political interest groups and process leading to formation
  of state and setting up of government machinery.

Republique Arabe de Libye, Ministere de la Culture et de
l'Information
La Revolution du 1er Septembre, Le Deuxieme Anniversaire
(Benghazi: Matati Dar-al-Haqiqa, 1971)

La Revolution du 1er Septembre, Le Quatrieme Anniversaire
(Benghazi: Matati Dar-al-Haqiqa, 1973)

3. Mauritania

GERTEINY, Alfred G.
Mauritania (London: Pall Mall Press, 1967)   243 pp.
Bibliography.

One of few works in English on Mauritania; studies all
aspects of nation, not only politics.

PIQUEMAL-PASTRE, Marcel
La Republique Islamique de Mauritanie (Encyclopedie
Politique et Constitutionnelle, Institut International
d'Administration Publique; Paris: Editions Berger-Levrault,
1969)   49 pp.
Bibliography.

Outlines plitical sociology, new and old political forces,
political evolution and current situation in terms of
politics and constitution. Includes text of constitution
of 1959 and modifications.

4. Morocco

ADAM, Andre
Casablanca: essai sur la transformation de la societe
marocaine au contact de l'Occident (Paris: 1968) 2 Vols.
895 pp.

Magistral study which documents and illuminates political
and social change.

ASHFORD, Douglas E.
Political Change in Morocco (Princeton, N.J.: Princeton
University Press, 1961)   432 pp.

Invaluable account of Moroccan nationalist movement and
politics of independence, although limited by perspective
of American political scientist.

AYACHE, Albert
Le Maroc (Paris: 1956)

Valuable survey of geography, economic resources and
politics of Morocco from nineteenth century to independence.

WATERBURY, John
The Commander of the Faithful (London: Weidenfeld & Nicolson, 1970) 366 pp.

Indispensable analysis of Moroccan politics, from independence to time of writing, which relates political behaviour to traditional political culture.

ZARTMAN, I. William
Problems of a New Power: Morocco (New York: Atherton Press, 1964) 276 pp.

Discusses evacuation of US bases, reorganization of army, agrarian reform, education and organization of elections.

5. Tunisia

DURUPTY, Michel
Institutions Administratives et Droit Administratif Tunisiens (Paris: Centre National de la Recherche Scientifique, 1973) 408 pp.
Bibliography.

Surveys structure of administration under French protectorate and then in independent Tunisia analyzes relationships between administration and judiciary. Documentary appendices.

KNAPP, Wilfrid
Tunisia (London: Thames & Hudson, 1970) 224 pp.

Survey with historical outline from earliest times to government and economics in Bourguiba's republic.

MICAUD, Charles, with Leon Carl BROWN and Clement Henry MOORE
Tunisia: the politics of modernization (London: 1964)

Collection of essays on origins of Tunisian nationalism, advent of independence and early years of independent government.

MOORE, Clement Henry
Tunisia since Independence (Berkeley: University of California Press, 1965) 230 pp.
Bibliography.

Systematic study of Tunisian politics concerned with such concepts as consensus and nation-building, based on detailed knowledge of personalities and political groupings.

PONCET, Jean
La Tunisie a la Recherche de Son Avenir: independance ou neocolonialisme? (Paris: 1974)

Critical left-wing account of Tunisian achievements since independence.

SEBAG, Paul
La Tunisie (Paris: Editions Sociales, 1951)

Valuable survey, written at time of independence from a Marxist viewpoint, replete with information.

C. POLITICAL PARTIES, INTEREST GROUPS AND IDEOLOGIES

DEBBAGCH, Charles
La Formation des Elites Politiques Maghrebines (Paris: R. Pichon et R. Durand-Auzias, 1973)   246 pp.

ETIENNE, Bruno
Les Problemes Juridiques des Minorites Europeennes au Maghreb (Paris: Centre National de la Recherche Scientifique, 1968)   414 pp.
Bibliography.

Elegant study derived from scrupulous interpretation of law and understanding of North African history which was, however, overtaken by departure of European population. Documentary appendices.

FANON, Frantz
Pour la Revolution Africaine (Paris: Francois Maspero, 1964)   223 pp.

Collection of articles and essays written between 1952-61; most of them already published but some articles (including those in El Moudjahid) not easily available.

GELLNER, Ernest, and Charles MICAUD, eds.
Arabs and Berbers (London: Duckworth, 1973)

Collection of essays on tribal organization and its importance in Algeria, Morocco and Mauritania in nineteenth and twentieth centuries. Many of contributions are of seminal importance.

MONTAGNE, Robert
The Berbers (London: Frank Cass, 1973)   93 pp.

Translation and introduction by David Seddon of French, La Vie Sociale et La Vie Politique des Berberes (Paris: Societe de l'Afrique Francaise, 1931). Preface by

Ernest Gellner. Brilliant account of Berber society.
Of cardinal importance for an understanding of protectorate policy.

PURTSCHET, Christian, and Andre VALENTINO
    Sociologie Electorale en Afrique du Nord (Paris: Presses
    Universitaires de France, 1966)   234 pp.

    Detailed survey of legislative elections in Algeria (1958)
    and Moroccan referendum of December 1962.

TEITLER, M., A. NOUSCHI, M. CAMAU, B. ETIENNE, N. SRAIEB, J.C.
SANTUCCI, J.J. REGNIER, O. MARAIS, J. LECA
    Elites, Pouvoir et Legitimite au Maghreb (Paris: Centre
    National de la Recherche Scientifique, 1973)   236 pp.

    Collection of articles drawn from Annuaire de l'Afrique
    du Nord which analyzes claim to legitimacy in Maghreb
    generally and in Tunisia and Algeria. Also includes
    articles on Jadiki College and Moroccan army.

ZARTMAN, I. William, ed.
    Man, State and Society in the Contemporary Maghrib
    (London: Pall Mall Press, 1973)   531 pp.
    Bibliography.

    Series of essays dealing with general characteristics of
    region (Morocco, Algeria, Tunsia, Libya), spectrum of
    values and attitudes, leaders and personalities, elites
    and social groups, political forces and institutions,
    changes required to dominate environment. Book especial-
    ly useful for those who read no French because includes
    many translations of articles originally written in
    French.

1. Algeria

CLEGG, Ian
    Workers' Self-Management in Algeria (London: Allen Lane,
    The Penguin Press, 1971)   249 pp.

    Describes ideological origins of 'autogestion', early
    legislation of Republic, and attempt at implementation.

DUCHEMIN, Jacques C.
    Histoire du F.L.N. (Paris: La Table Ronde, 1962) 327 pp.

    Episodic history of Algerian nationalist movement. First
    part traces background before 1954; remainder a somewhat
    uncritical account of war years.

MERAD, Ali
Ibn Badis: commentateur du Coran (Algiers: 1971)

Account of political and religious thought of founder of
Ulema movement.

QUANDT, William B.
Revolution and Political Leadership in Algeria 1954-68
(Cambridge, Mass.: Harvard University Press, 1969)

Best analytical account of rivalries within Algerian
leadership.

TREBOUS, Madeleine
Migration and Development (Paris: OECD, 1970)   242 pp.

Surveys employment training in Algeria, stages and features of emigration, distribution of Algerian labour in
Europe, and problems which arise therefrom. Suggests
'tentative solutions'.

2. Libya

NORMAN, John
Labour and Politics in Libya and Arab Africa   (New York:
Bookman, 1965)   219 pp.

Rare study of North African, but especially Libyan labour,
concerned with internal organization and disputes and
external relations, especially with ICFTU.

4. Morocco

BERQUE, Jacques
Structures Sociales du Haut-Atlas (Paris: Presses Universitaires de France, 1955)   470 pp.

Anthropological study of tribal and village society of
Seksawa.

CAMAU, Michel
Le Notion de Democratie dans la Pensee des Dirigeants
Marocains (Paris: Centre National de la Recherche Sci-
entifique, 1971)   502 pp.
Bibliography.

Analysis of theories of state, nation, liberty, Marxist
ideas, etc. as expressed in political discourse of
North Africa.

GEERTZ, Clifford
 <u>Islam Observed</u>   (New Haven: Yale University Press, 1968)
 136 pp.

Comparative account of practice of Islam in Indonesia
and Morocco based on extended anthropological field work.

GELLNER, Ernest
 <u>Saints of the Atlas</u>   (London: 1969)

Seminal anthropological study of tribal structure, especially part played by holy men in Atlas mountains.

HALSTEAD, John P.
 <u>Rebirth of a Nation: the origins and rise of Moroccan
 nationalism 1912-44</u>   (Cambridge, Mass.: Harvard University Press, 1967)   323 pp.

NOIN, Daniel
 <u>La Population Rurale du Maroc</u>   (Paris: Presses Universitaires de France, 1970)   2 Vols.

Detailed survey of its subject which thus provides context of political organization in countryside.

REZETTE, Robert
 <u>Les Partis Politiques Marocains</u>   (Paris: Fondation
 National des Sciences Politiques, 1955)   404 pp.

Informative and descriptive account of Moroccan political
parties.

5. Tunisia

BARDIN, Pierre
 <u>La Vie d'un Douar</u>   (Paris/La Haye: Mouton, 1965)

Vivid sociological study of Tunisian hamlet in Medjerda
valley.

BELING, Willard
 <u>Modernization and African Labour: a Tunisian case study</u>
 (New York: Praeger, 1965)

Valuable as an historical and institutional account of
Tunisian trade union movement.

DUVIGNAUD, Jean
 <u>Chebika</u>   (Paris: 1968)

Sensitive account of decline in village in south of
Tunisia.

RUDEBECK, Lars
> Party and People   (Uppsala, Sweden: Almquist & Wiksells, 1967)   275 pp.

> Monograph based in part on empirical research in Tunisia, showing attitudes to political and social questions.

D. BIOGRAPHIES, MEMOIRS, SPEECHES, WRITINGS BY POLITICAL LEADERS

LACOUTURE, Jean
> Cinq Hommes et la France   (Paris: Editions du Seuil, 1961)   371 pp.

> Journalist's study of five leaders in former French colonies: Ho Chi Minh (Vietnam), Habib Bourguiba (Tunisia), Mohammed V (Morocco), Ferhat Abbas (Algeria), and Sekou Toure (Guinea). Based on author's personal contact with them and considerable knowledge of countries concerned; emphasizes relations of each leader with French during periods leading to independence.

1. Algeria

ABBAS, Ferhat
> Guerre et Revolution d'Algerie; I. La Nuit Coloniale (Paris: Julliard, 1962)   233 pp.

> Account of French rule in Algeria by nationalist leader who argues the injustices of 'colonial' rule.

BENNABI, Malek
> Memoires d'un Temoin du Siecle   (Algiers: 1965)

> Rare political memoir of Algerian politics in interwar years, including Muslim perspectives of European settlers.

BOUDIAF, Mohammed
> Ou Va l'Algerie?   (Paris: 1964)

> View of Algeria by left-wing participant in independence movement who then went into opposition.

CHALLE, Maurice
> Notre Revolte   (Paris: Presses de la Cite, 1968)   443 pp.

> Collection of notes and commentaries on Algerian war and on various aspects of French foreign policy, etc. to 1965, by leader of abortive officers' coup against de Gaulle in 1961.

FANON, Frantz
   Sociologie d'une Revolution: l'an V de la revolution
   africaine (Paris: Francois Maspero, 1966)

   Expresses author's hopes and aspirations for Algerian
   revolution.

FERAOUN, Mouloud
   Journal 1955-62 (Paris: Editions du Seuil, 1962) 348 pp.

   Diary of Algerian schoolmaster who was killed at end of
   war; sensitive and detached account.

LEBJAOUI, Mohammed
   Bataille d'Alger ou Bataille d'Algerie (Paris: Gallimard,
   1972) 301 pp.

   Memoirs of battle of Algiers. Documentary appendix.

LEBJAOUI, Mohammed
   Verites sur la Revolution Algerienne (Paris: Gallimard,
   1970) 249 pp.

   Memoirs of Algerian nationalist movement by participant.

MERLE, Robert
   Ben Bella (London: Michael Joseph, 1965)   160 pp.

   Translated from French, Ahmed Ben Bella (Paris: Gallimard, 1965). An author's preface precedes Ben Bella's
   own souvenirs which Merle edited and published shortly
   after Ben Bella's fall in 1965.

SALAN, Raoul
   Memoires: fin d'un empire (Paris: Presses de la Cite,
   1972) 4 Vols.

   Volumes 3 and 4 of author's memoirs cover period of his
   command in Algeria from 1954 to 1958. Documentary
   appendix.

SERVAN-SCHREIBER, Jean Jacques
   Lieutenant in Algeria (London: Hutchinson, 1958)
   206 pp.

   Recounts personal experiences of author (editor of
   L'Express) serving in Algeria. Original French edition
   was important in giving reality to the war and raising
   critical questions about its purpose and outcome.

2. Libya

BIANCO, Mirella
Kadhafi: messages du desert (Paris: Editions Stock,
1974)   318 pp.

English edition, Gadafi: voice from the desert (Paris:
1975). Biographical study by Italian writer based on
extensive interviews with Libyan leader.

QADHDHAFI, Colonel Mu'ammar al-
Le Receuil (National) des Discours, Allocutions, Inter-
views et Propos du Colonel Mu'ammar al-Qadhahafi
(Tripoli: Publications de l'USA, 1970-73) 4 Vols.

QADHDHAFI, Colonel Mu'ammar al-
La Revolution du Peuple Arabe de Libye, d'apres les
Propos du Frere Colonel Mu'ammar al-Qadhdhafi (Tripoli:
Imprimeries de la Revolution Arabe, 1972-73) 2 Vols.

4. Morocco

BEN BARKA, Mehdi
Option Revolutionnaire au Maroc (Paris: Francois Maspero, 1966)   159 pp.

Most useful collection of views of outstanding opposition
leader published after his disappearance in 1965.

EL-ALAMI, Mohammed
Allal al-Fassi (Paris: 1972; Rabat: Arrissala, 1972)
252 pp.

Political biography principally concerned with al-Fassi's
leadership of Istiqlal party.

GAUDIO, Attilio
Allal al-Fassi ou l'Histoire de l'Istiqlal (Rabat:
Moreau, 1972)   365 pp.

Studies early life, analysis of political and economic
vies, attitude of Istiqlal to Sahara question.

HASSAN II, King
Le Maroc en Marche (Rabat: 1965)   541 pp.

Selection of king's speeches from his accession (1961)
to 1965.

HOWE, Sonia E.
Lyautey of Morocco: an authorized life (London: Hodder
& Stoughton, 1931)   338 pp.
Bibliography.

Book deals with all of Marshal Lyautey's activities, especially his contributions in Morocco. Positive view.

LYAUTEY, Pierre
Lyautey L'Africain: textes et lettres du Marechal Lyautey (Paris: Librairie Plon, 1953) 4 Vols.

Each volume covers separate period: 1912-13, 1913-15, 1915-18, 1919-25.

MAUROIS, Andre
Marshal Lyautey (London: Bodley Head, 1931)   290 pp.

Biography of Lyautey during his rule in Morocco.

5. Tunisia

NERFIN, Marc
Entretiens avec Ahmed ben Salah (Paris: Francois Maspero, 1974)   198 pp.

Introduction followed by reminiscences and commentary by ben Salah on Tunisian politics and economics from independence to fall of ben Salah.

E. EXTERNAL RELATIONS

GALLAGHER, Charles
The United States and North Africa: Morocco, Algeria and Tunisia (Cambridge, Mass.: Harvard University Press, 1963)   275 pp.

Historical account of United States relations with the Maghreb which provides invaluable insight into politics and economics of region.

GASTEYGER, C., R. ALIBONI, C. TNANI, A. LAMANNA, J.-J. BERREBY, D. PEPY, A. CHANDERLI
Europe and the Maghreb (Paris: The Atlantic Institute, 1972)   72 pp.

Series of short papers which are now primarily of historical interest.

4. Morocco

CONSTANT, Jean-Paul
Les Relations Maroco-Sovietique 1956-71 (Paris: R. Pichon and R. Durand-Auzias, 1973)   136 pp.

Exhaustive study of diplomatic economic aid relationship.

HALL, Luella J.
The United States and Morocco 1776-1956   (Metuchen, N.J.:
Scarecrow Press, 1971)   1114 pp.

Exhaustive study, from problem of piracy to World War II
and advent of independence. Notable for its detail
rather than structure or analysis.

REZETTE, Robert
Le Sahara et les Frontieres Marocaines   (Paris: Nouvelles
Editions Latines, 1975)   188 pp.

Historical survey, touching Middle Ages and ending with
submission of Saharan question to International Court.
Sceptical of self-determination, argues Moroccan case.

TROUT, Frank E.
Morocco's Saharan Frontiers   (Geneva: Drog Publishers,
1969)   561 pp.
Bibliography.

Historical and legal survey of frontiers from 1845 to
time of writing, which stresses sources of tension with
Algeria. Includes maps.

MIDDLE EAST - GENERAL

A. POLITICAL HISTORY

BERQUE, Jacques
  The Arabs: their history and future (London: 1964)

  Translated from French, Les Arabes d'Hier a Demain
  (Paris: Editions du Seuil, 1960). Revised edition in
  French (Paris: Editions du Seuil, 1969). Sensitive account of Arab civilization, politics and culture, close-
  ly interwoven; drawing on author's wide knowledge and
  perception of relationships between history, morals,
  customs, economics and politics.

KIRK, G.E.
  A Short History of the Middle East: from the rise of
  Islam to modern times (London: Methuen, 1964) Seventh
  edition. 340 pp.

  About half of book is concerned with 20th century, with
  study of Russian involvement and revolution in Middle
  East.

POLK, William R., and Richard L. CHAMBERS, eds.
  Beginnings of Modernization in the Middle East: the
  nineteenth century (Chicago: University of Chicago
  Press, 1968) 427 pp.

  Centres on Ottoman reforms of 19th century and their
  spread through Egypt, Syria and Sudan.

B. POLITICAL SYSTEMS, GOVERNMENT

ABBOUSHI, W.F.
  Political Systems of the Middle East in the Twentieth
  Century (New York: 1970)

  Standard and valuable introduction.

ADAMS, Michael, ed.
  The Middle East: a handbook (London: A. Blond, 1971)
  633 pp.

  Comprehensive handbook treats general background and
  individual countries: politics, economics, social and

cultural affairs. Very detailed with tables.

BERGER, Morroe
The Arab World Today (London: 1962)

Analytical survey which provides excellent introduction
to constituents of Arab politics, religious thought and
practice, and social customs.

HALPERN, Manfred
The Politics of Social Change in the Middle East and
North Africa (Princeton, N.J.: Princeton University
Press, 1963)   431 pp.

Considers material from Morocco, Algeria, Tunisia, Libya,
Egypt, Sudan, Jordan, Saudi Arabia, Yemen, Lebanon,
Syria, Iraq, Turkey, Afghanistan, Pakistan. Discusses
aspects of inheritance of Islamic community, changing
structure of society, range of political choices, instruments of political modernization, cost and consequences
of Middle Eastern choices.

LANDAU, Jacob M., ed.
Man, State and Society in the Contemporary Middle East
(London: Pall Mall Press, 1972)

Collection of articles and essays of high quality on
various aspects of Middle Eastern politics.

LERNER, Daniel, and Lucille W. PEVSNER
The Passing of Traditional Society: modernizing the
Middle East (Illinois: Glencoe Free Press, 1958)
466 pp.

Much recommended text, well researched. Continuing
theory of modernization with considerable detail on
Turkey, Lebanon, Egypt, Syria, Jordan and Iran.

PERETZ, Don
The Middle East Today (New York: 1963)   495 pp.

Introductory study emphasizing various common strands of
development. Very full chapters on each of countries.

SHARABI, Hisham B.
Government and Politics of the Middle East in the Twen-
tieth Century (Princeton, N.J.: Princeton University
Press, 1962)   290 pp.

Fairly standard handbook, with background and country-
by-country analysis.

VATIKIOTIS, P.J., ed.
   Revolution in the Middle East   (London: George Allen &
   Unwin, 1972)   232 pp.

   Political/historical approach to concept and evidence of
   'revolution' in Middle East region; each author sets his
   own theoretical framework for discussion of his particular concern; discusses both attitudes and action regarding existence of revolution; examines validity of apply-
   ing Western concepts of revolution to recent upheavals
   in Middle East; finally, contrasts situation in Middle
   East with that in Eastern Europe, Latin America and China.

C. POLITICAL PARTIES, INTEREST GROUPS AND IDEOLOGIES

ABDEL-MALEK, Anwar
   La Pensee Politique Arabe Contemporaine   (Paris: Editions
   du Seuil, 1970)   378 pp.
   Bibliography.

   Useful introduction to subject, especially its account
   of Arab nationalism and socialism.

ANTONIUS, George
   The Arab Awakening: the story of the Arab national movement   (London: 1955)

   Account of rise of Arab nationalism in 19th and 20th centuries which has become classic. Appendix prints documents from diplomacy of World War I, including MacMahon
   correspondence.

ANTOUN, R., and I. HARIK, eds.
   Rural Politics and Social Change in the Middle East
   (Bloomington: University of Indiana Press, 1972)

   Valuable collection of essays which provide sociological
   background to political development.

BE'ERI, Eliezer
   Army Officers in Arab Politics and Society   (London:
   1970)

   Sociological account of background and role of military
   in Arab world.

BINDER, Leonard
   The Ideological Revolution in the Middle East   (New York:
   John Wiley & Sons, 1964)   287 pp.

   Interpretative account of traditionalism and modernization with emphasis on nationalism and Nasserism.

HAIM, Sylvia G., ed.
Arab Nationalism: an anthology (Berkeley/Los Angeles:
University of California Press, 1964)   255 pp.
Bibliography.

Editor's valuable introduction comprises first 70 pp. and
relates nationalism to other trends in Middle East: politics, Islam, etc. Remainder of book includes selections
from Arab writers on nationalism chosen for their historical importance or because they represent important current of opinion; writers include such leaders as Negib
Azoury, Sami Shawkat, Charles Malik, Nasser, Michel
Aflaq, etc.

HOURANI, Albert
Arabic Thought in the Liberal Age 1789-1939 (London:
Oxford University Press, 1960)   390 pp.

Authoritative study of its subject which informs about
more recent movement towards modernization.

HUREWITZ, J.C.
Middle East Politics: the military dimension (London:
Pall Mall Press, 1969)   553 pp.
Bibliography.

Standard approach. Good both on country-by-country description and general study.

LAQUER, Walter Z.
Communism and Nationalism in the Middle East (London:
Routledge & Kegan Paul, 1955)   362 pp.

First and still the major study of history of communism
in Middle East and its relation to Arab nationalism.

LAROUI, Abdallah
L'Ideologie Arabe Contemporaine (Paris: Francois Maspero,
1967)   221 pp.

Preface by Maxime Rodinson. Sensitive and reflective
critical essay by Moroccan historian.

NUSEIBEH, Hazem Zaki
The Ideas of Arab Nationalism (Ithaca, N.Y.: Cornell
University Press, 1956)   226 pp.

Full study of background, ideology and role of Arab nationalism. Emphasizes strong links with Islam.

SAYEGH, Fayez A.
  Arab Unity, Hope and Fulfillment   (New York: Devin-Adair,
  1958)

  Evaluative study of idea of Arab unity, Ba'ath Party and
  Arab League, ending with hopes for future.

SHARABI, Hisham B.
  Nationalism and Revolution in the Arab World   (Princeton,
  N.J.: Princeton University Press, 1966)   175 pp.

  Divided into two sections: (1) set of chapters under
  general title of book; (2) speeches, resolutions, ideologies and statements made in course of various coups
  d'etat.

VATIKIOTIS, P.J.
  Conflict in the Middle East   (London: George Allen &
  Unwin, 1971)   224 pp.

  As its title: Great Power involvement, internal struggle,
  and Israeli problem, with some insight into problem of
  guerillas.

VON GRUNEBAUM, G.E., ed.
  Unity and Variety in Muslim Civilization   (Chicago: University of Chicago Press, 1955)   383 pp.

  Collection of essays emphasizing study of Islam, but also
  including chapters on evolution of Iran, Turkey, and on
  'body politic'. Useful for comprehensive view of Islam
  and its effects.

E. EXTERNAL RELATIONS (INTERNATIONAL POLITICS WHOSE CONCERN IS
PRIMARILY ARAB AND AFRICAN STATES)

BADEAU, John S.
  The American Approach to the Arab World   (New York: 1968)

  Valuable perception of US diplomat who served in Egypt
  during Yemen war.

LAQUER, Walter Z.
  The Soviet Union and the Middle East   (New York: Praeger,
  1959)   366 pp.

  Divided into two parts: (1) from 1920 to Stalin's death;
  (2) from 1954-58. Covers both Soviet view of Middle
  East and history of its direct actions in Middle East;
  includes some general chapters on communism, aid and
  Arab nationalism.

LEWIS, Bernard
    The Middle East and the West (London: 1964)   164 pp.

    Short general history of meeting of two cultures and its
    effects.

MACDONALD, Robert W.
    The League of Arab States: a study in the dynamics of
    regional organization (Princeton, N.J.: Princeton Univ-
    ersity Press, 1965)

    Standard account of history and organization of Arab
    League.

MOSELY, Leonard
    Power Play, The Tumultuous World of Middle East Oil:
    1890-1973 (London: Weidenfeld & Nicolson, 1973) 374 pp.
    Bibliography.

    Lively and entertaining account of development of Middle
    Eastern oil industry by well-known British author who
    has based his account largely on interviews with leading
    personalities in oil companies and oil-producing states.

World Energy Demands and the Middle East (Proceedings of 26th
    Annual Conference; Washington, D.C.: The Middle East
    Institute, 1972)   162 pp.

    Collection of papers and addresses by specialists on
    Middle East and energy-related problems from academic,
    government, business and financial communities. Includes
    transcripts of addresses by Sheikh Yamani (Saudi Arabian
    Minister of Petroleum) and James E. Akins (US Dept. of
    State). Plenary sessions and special panels examined
    such topics as pressures of energy demands on resources,
    politics of oil demand and supply, prospects for cooper-
    ation between oil producers, implications of spiraling
    energy demands on future of Middle East; preparing for
    economic diversification: internal political, economic
    and social policies, etc.

ARAB MIDDLE EAST AND SUDAN

BAER, Gabriel
A History of Landownership in Modern Egypt 1800-1950
(for Royal Institute of International Affairs; London:
Oxford University Press, 1962)   255 pp.
Bibliography.

Well-documented study of stages in landownership from
development of private ownership to formation of large
estates in 19th century, disintegration of large estates
and evolution of Waqf system; concludes with discussion
of various points of view regarding land reform before
military revolution.   Includes many appendices and tables.

BAER, Gabriel
Studies in the Social History of Modern Egypt   (Chicago:
University of Chicago Press, 1969)   259 pp.

Series of studies concerning problems arising from transformation of medieval Islamic society to something new
but undefined.   Considers problem of peasant: his community, his leaders, his land, his religious organization, his attitudes; studies development of penal code
for restraining social violence; treats growth of urban
society in terms of its government, laws, slavery;
provides summary conclusion of period from 1800-1914.

BERQUE, Jacques
Egypt: imperialism and revolution   (London: Faber &
Faber, 1972)   736 pp.

Translation of French edition (Paris: Gallimard, 1967).
Historical account leading up to revolution of 1952
showing Egyptian response to imperial rule.   Invaluable
for insights drawn from Egyptian sources.

HOLT, P.M., ed.
Political and Social Change in Modern Egypt   (London:
Oxford University Press, 1968)   400 pp.

Historical studies from Ottoman conquest to United Arab
Republic; studies in source materials could be of special
relevance to research students; authors are all well-
known experts on Egypt or are Egyptians themselves.

LITTLE, Tom
Modern Egypt   (London: Benn, 1967)

Wide-ranging historical survey which gives excellent
general perspective to Nasser's Egypt.

VATIKIOTIS, P.J.
The Modern History of Egypt   (London: Weidenfeld & Nicolson, 1969)   512 pp.

Comprehensive historical survey from 1805 to 1962.

2. Iraq

DANN, Uriel
Iraq under Qassem: a political history 1958-63   (Jerusalem: 1969)

Useful survey of its subject.

KHADDURI, Majid
Independent Iraq 1932-58   (London: Oxford University
Press, 1960)   Second edition.

Standard political history based on personal observation
and interviews as well as published sources.

LONGRIGG, Stephen H., and Frank STOAKES
Iraq   (London: Benn, 1958)   264 pp.

Readable survey, historical in plan, covering major
aspects of Iraq at time of Nuri as Said.

LONGRIGG, Stephen H.
Iraq 1900-50   (London: Oxford University Press, 1953)
436 pp.

Detailed, well-informed political, social and economic
history.

3. Jordan

MORRIS, James
> The Hashemite Kings   (London: Faber & Faber, 1959)
> 231 pp.

Studies King Hussein of the Hejaz and his descendants
who ruled Jordan and Iraq.

PEAKE, Frederick G.
> History and Tribes of Jordan   (Florida: Miami University
> Press, 1958)252 pp.

Mainly concerns Bedouin and tribal system, with some
modern (20th century) history.

4. Lebanon

AGWANI, M.S.
> The Lebanese Crisis 1958: a documentary study   (London:
> Asia Publishing House, 1965)   407 pp.

Substantial collection of public speeches and documents,
Lebanese and foreign, with brief commentary.

HITTI, Philip K.
> A Short History of Lebanon   (New York: Macmillan, 1965)
> 248 pp.

Covers history of area from earliest days. Superficial
account of recent history, directed to general readership.

HOURANI, Albert H.
> Syria and Lebanon: a political essay   (Oxford: 1946)
> 402 pp.

Historical examination of French mandate, illuminated by
reflective view of relation between Arab world and West.

QUBAIN, Fahim I.
> Crisis in Lebanon   (Washington, D.C.: Middle East Insti-
> tute, 1961)   244 pp.

Study of origins, course and settlement of crisis of 1958.

SALIBI, Kamal S.
> The Modern History of Lebanon   (London: Weidenfeld &
> Nicolson, 1965)   228 pp.

Provides history from beginning of Shihal Emirate (c.
1700) to 1958. Detailed and concise; especially lucid
analysis of confessional question.

5. Sudan

ABBAS, Mekki
The Sudan Question: the dispute over the Anglo-Egyptian
Condominium (London: Faber & Faber, 1952)   201 pp.

General political survey by distinguished Sudanese
teacher.

ABD AL-RAHIM, Muddathir
Imperialism and Nationalism in the Sudan: a study in
constitutional and political development (Oxford: Clarendon Press, 1969)   275 pp.

A scholarly and comprehensive account; documentary appendices and bibliography.

BESHIR, Mohamed Omer
The Southern Sudan (London: Hurst, 1968)   192 pp.

Historical survey from 1898 to time of writing; documentary appendix.

DUNCAN, J.S.R.
The Sudan's Path to Independence (London: Blackwood,
1957)   231 pp.

General political account by former member of Sudan
political service.

FABUNMI, L.A.
The Sudan in Anglo-Egyptian Relations (London: Longmans,
1960)   451 pp.

Traces impact of Anglo-Egyptian relations on political
development of Sudan from 1800-1956.

NASRI, Adel Rahman el
A Bibliography of the Sudan 1938-58 (London: Oxford
University Press, 1962)   171 pp.

SAID, Beshir Mohammed
The Sudan: crossroads of Africa (London: Bodley Head,
1965)   238 pp.

Critical account of British and Sudanese administration
and impact of missionaries, particularly with reference
to Southern Sudan. Documentary appendices.

SHIBEIKA, Mekki
The Independent Sudan (New York: Speller, 1959)   506 pp.

Largely historical account with final chapters on movement to independence.

6. Syria

SEALE, P.
The Struggle for Syria: a study of post-war Arab politics
1945-58 (London: Oxford University Press, 1965)   344 pp.

Detailed and well-informed account of Syrian politics
under impact of international diplomacy.

TIBAWI, A.L.
A Modern History of Syria   (London: Macmillan, 1969)
441 pp.
Bibliography.

Political history of geographical Syria (including Lebanon and Palestine) from end of 18th century to settlement
following World War I.

B. POLITICAL SYSTEMS, GOVERNMENT

1. Egypt

BERGER, Morroe
Bureaucracy and Society in Modern Egypt   (Princeton, N.J.:
Princeton University Press, 1957)

Useful specialist study which throws light on Egyptian
political development at time of writing.

DEKMEJIAN, R. Hrair
Egypt under Nasser   (Albany: State University of New York
Press, 1971)

Valuable analysis of impact of Nasser's presidency on
internal politics, economy and society of Egypt, and its
foreign relations.

HOPKINS, Harry
Egypt the Crucible: the unfinished revolution of the
Arab world   (London: Secker & Warburg, 1969) 533 pp.
Bibliography.

Attempt to present reappraisal of Arab world: its social
revolution and changing circumstances; focuses on Egypt
from beginning of revolution; reassessment considered
important by author also in terms of Arab world vis-a-
vis Israel.

MANSFIELD, Peter
> Nasser's Egypt (Harmondsworth, Middlesex: Penguin Afri-
> can Library, Penguin Books, 1965)   222 pp.
>
> Political history of Egypt centering on Nasser's rise to
> power and his governmental policies; discusses interna-
> tional relations with other Arab states and with East/
> West powers; explains Nasser's economic policies and
> political system that evolved after revolution.

O'BRIEN, Patrick K.
> The Revolution in Egypt's Economic System: from private
> enterprise to socialism 1952-65 (London: Oxford Univer-
> sity Press, 1966)
>
> Work of economic history which is also important for its
> political implications.

2. Iraq

KHADDURI, Majid
> Republican Iraq: a study in Iraqi politics since the
> revolution of 1958 (London: Oxford University Press,
> 1970)   318 pp.
>
> Best political study available on developments during
> decade following overthrow of monarchy; based on author's
> long familiarity with events in Iraq and his extensive
> interviews with various members of Iraqi elite.

QUBAIN, Fahim I.
> The Reconstruction of Iraq 1950-57 (London: Atlantic
> Books, 1958; New York: Praeger, 1958)   277 pp.
>
> Factual survey of economic base: agriculture, oil, in-
> dustry, human resources.

VERNIER, Bernard
> L'Irak d'Aujourd'hui (Paris: Armand Colin, 1963) 494 pp.
>
> General survey: historical introduction preceding main
> study of politics, foreign relations and Kurdish question
> from 1958 to time of writing.

3. Jordan

ABIDI, Aqil H.H.
> Jordan: a political study 1948-57 (London: Asia Pub-
> lishing House, 1965)   251 pp.
>
> General survey, useful in default of more recent and
> fundamental work.

DEARDEN, Ann
   Jordan (London: Hale, 1958)   224 pp.

   General survey whose value diminishes with passage of
   time.

HARRIS, G.L.
   Jordan: its people, its society, its culture   (New Haven:
   Yale University Press, 1958)   246 pp.

   Factual account of Jordan's physical and geographical
   features and a somewhat superficial overview of politics.

PATAI, R.
   The Kingdom of Jordan (Princeton, N.J.: Princeton University Press, 1958)   301 pp.

   General, balanced study of all aspects of Jordan.

SHWADRAN, Benjamin
   Jordan: a state of tension   (New York: Council for Middle
   Eastern Affairs Press, 1959)   436 pp.
   Bibliography.

   General survey, now somewhat dated.

4. Lebanon

HUDSON, Michael C.
   The Precarious Republic: political modernization in
   Lebanon (New York: Random House, 1968)   364 pp.
   Bibliography.

   Valuable study of Lebanese politics. Divided into four
   sections: introduction; stresses and destabilizing ten-
   dencies; political actors; institutional performance.

SALEM, Elie Adeb
   Modernization without Revolution: Lebanon's experience
   (Bloomington: University of Indiana Press, 1973)

   Account limited to bureaucratic reform and development
   planning which provides useful insights.

5. Sudan

ALBINO, Oliver
   The Sudan: a southern viewpoint   (London: Oxford University Press, 1970)   132 pp.

   Foreword by Arnold Toynbee. Opens with history of Sudan
   and analysis of southern question; recounts author's
   experience which led to his exile; personal notes on
   Round Table Conference.

BESHIR, Mohamed Omer
Revolution and Nationalism in the Sudan   (London: Rex
Collings, 1974)   314 pp.
Bibliography.

Covers historical experience and modern politics, con-
cluding with chapter on coup d'etat and revolution 1956-
64.

HENDERSON, K.D.D.
Sudan Republic   (London: Benn, 1965)   233 pp.

General historical/political survey.   Successor to
Macmichael (see below).

HOLT, Peter M.
A Modern History of the Sudan: from the Funji Sultanate
to the present day   (London: Weidenfeld & Nicolson,
1961)   242 pp.
Bibliography.

Standard work by leading authority.

MACMICHAEL, Sir Harold
The Sudan   (London: Benn, 1954)

General historical and political survey by former governor of Sudan.

Ministry of Information and Culture, Khartoum
The Sudan Today   (Nairobi and Tavistock (UK): University
Press of Africa, n.d.)   234 pp.

WAI, Dunstan M.
The Southern Sudan: the problem of integration   (London:
Frank Cass, 1973)   255 pp.

Collection of essays covering race relations, economics,
education and political trends.   Documentary appendix.

6. Syria

ZIADEH, Nicola A.
Syria and Lebanon   (London: 1957)   300 pp.

Very general picture: land, history, economy, etc.

C. POLITICAL PARTIES, INTEREST GROUPS AND IDEOLOGIES

1. Egypt

BERGER, Morroe
Islam in Egypt Today: social and political aspects of
popular religion   (Cambridge: Cambridge University Press,
1970)   138 pp.
Bibliography.

Discusses nature of Islamic government and voluntary
associations; describes some aspects of religious organization in Egypt today including organization of mosques
and governments use of religion in its own policies;
considers Sufi organization and activity; analyzes Egyptian voluntary religious associations and their social
activities. For lack of adequate data, not all sections
are well-documented but observations are very useful;
some data comes from previously unknown governmental
studies.

BERGER, Morroe
Military Elite and Social Change: Egypt since Napoleon
(Princeton, N.J.: Princeton University Press, 1960)

Wide ranging view of the subject.

DEKMEJIAN, R. Hrair
Patterns of Political Leadership: Egypt, Israel, Lebanon
(Albany: State University of New York Press, 1975) 323 pp.
Bibliography.

Unusual comparative study of origins, style and norms of
political leadership in Middle East.

LACOUTURE, Jean and Simonne
L'Egypte en Mouvement   (Paris: Editions du Seuil, 1956)
476 pp.

Vivid journalistic account: opens with historical introduction, followed by survey of village economy, dominance
of Cairo, nationalism and Islam in Nasser's Egypt.

MITCHELL, R.P.
The Society of the Muslim Brothers   (London: Oxford University Press, 1969)   349 pp.

Comprehensive examination of history, organization and
ideas of movement from its foundation (1928) to suppres-
sion by Nasser (1968).

SAID, Abdel Maghny
Arab Socialism   (London: Blandford Press, 1972)   137 pp.

With section by Samir Ahmed. Devoted almost entirely to
Egyptian socialism in Nasser period. Valuable as native
Egyptian contribution to subject, but lacking critical
perspective.

ZIADEH, Farhat J.
Lawyers, the Rule of Law,and Liberalism in Modern Egypt
(Stanford, Calif.: Hoover Institution Press, 1968) 177 pp.
Bibliography.

Describes rise of Western-oriented lawyers in Egypt to
dominant roles in public life until revolution in 1952
when basic changes in power structure relegated them to
role of legal technicians under military regime; analyzes
ramifications of 'rule of law' established by these lawyers and its long term effects on Egyptian system.

2. Iraq

ADAMSON, David
The Kurdish War   (London: George Allen & Unwin, 1964)
215 pp.

Personal narrative with limited political insight.

O'BALLANCE, Edgar
The Kurdish Revolt 1961-70   (London: Faber & Faber, 1973)
196 pp.

Critical narrative with special interest in war itself;
based on visit to Kurdistan and interviews with Iraqi
Arabs and Kurds.

JALAL, Ferhang
Role of Government in the Industrialization of Iraq 1950-
65 (London: Frank Cass, 1972)   229 pp.

Monograph by Director General of Industrial Bank of Iraq,
with historical introduction.

PRADIER, Jean
Les Kurdes: revolution silencieuse   (Bordeaux: Ducros,
1968)   286 pp.
Bibliography.

Work of reportage and reflection rather than analysis,
based on personal experience in Kurdistan.

3. Jordan

VATIKIOTIS, P.J.
> Politics and the Military in Jordan: a study of the Arab
> Legion 1921-57 (London: Frank Cass, 1967)   169 pp.

> Combines two separate studies - of Jordanian politics
> and of Arab Legion - with two concluding chapters dealing
> with them together.

4. Lebanon

BINDER, Leonard, ed.
> Politics in Lebanon (New York: John Wiley & Sons, 1966)
> 345 pp.

> Best single collection of essays covering major aspects
> of national balance, political parties, communal organi-
> zation, and religion in politics.

SULEIMAN, M.
> Political Parties in Lebanon (Ithaca, N.Y.: Cornell Uni-
> versity Press, 1967)   326 pp.

> Good background; well set out into types of political
> parties; detailed analysis of all parties; rather brief
> on future course of politics and trends in development
> of parties.

5. Sudan

EPRILE, Cecil
> War and Peace in the Sudan (London: David & Charles,
> 1974)   192 pp.
> Bibliography.

> Somewhat superficial account of political divisions and
> war in Sudan, with two chapters on Russian interest.

6. Syria

ABU JABER, Kemal S.
> The Arab Ba'ath Socialist Party (Syracuse: Syracuse
> University Press, 1966)

> Standard survey of the subject.

RABINOVICH, Itamar
> Syria under the Ba'ath 1961-63 (Jerusalem: Israeli
> Universities Press, 1975)

> Substantial analysis of organization of Syrian Ba'ath
> Party and its achievements over limited period.

TORREY, Gordon H.
    Syrian Politics and the Military 1945-58   (Ohio: Ohio
    State University Press, 1964)   431 pp.

    Considerable detail surrounding main topic. Well set out.

D. BIOGRAPHIES, MEMOIRS, SPEECHES, WRITINGS
BY POLITICAL LEADERS

1. Egypt

LACOUTURE, Jean
    The Demigods: charismatic leadership in the Third World
    (London: Secker & Warburg, 1970)   300 pp.

    Translated from French, Quatres Hommes et leurs Peuples
    (Paris: Editions du Seuil, 1969). Introduction discusses
    nature of charismatic leadership, its relation to author-
    ity, identity, etc. Four case studies including Bourguiba,
    Sihanouk, Nkrumah, Nasser, compared.

LACOUTURE, Jean
    Nasser   (Harmondsworth, Middlesex: Penguin Books, 1973)

    Translation of Nasser (Paris: Editions du Seuil, 1971).
    Biography written under impact of international events
    of Middle East; explores concept of Nasserism and rela-
    tions between Arab states and Israel.

NASSER, Gamal Abdel
    Egypt's Liberation: the philosophy of the revolution
    (Washington, D.C.: Public Affairs Press, 1955)

    Philosophy of revolution as expounded by leader of
    Egypt's revolution; an attempt to analyze himself and
    others who led revolution to discover what their role
    was to be in Egypt's history; attempt to formulate objec-
    tives and to measure resources, to analyze national en-
    vironment.

NASSER, Gamal Abdel
    Speeches and Press Interviews   (Cairo: United Arab Repub-
    lic Ministry of Information)

Vol. I	442 pp.	1958
Vol. II	626 pp.	1959
Vol. III	160 pp.	Jan.-Mar. 1960
Vol. IV	169 pp.	Apr.-June 1960
Vol. V	196 pp.	Oct.-Dec. 1960
Vol. VI	413 pp.	1961

NEGUIB, Mohammed
    Egypt's Destiny (London: Gollancz, 1955)
    Autobiography.

SADAT, Anwar el
    Revolte sur le Nil (Paris: Amiot, 1957)   219 pp.

    Preface by President Nasser. Personal and political
    reminiscences and reflections.

STEPHENS, R.
    Nasser: a political biography (London: 1971)
    Standard balanced biography.

2. Iraq

BIRDWOOD, Lord
    Nuri as-Said: a study in Arab leadership (London: 1959)
    Standard biography based on personal acquaintance.

3. Jordan

HUSSEIN, King of Jordan
    My War with Israel (London: Owen, 1969)   170 pp.

    As told to and with additional material by Vick Vance
    and Pierre Lauer (translated from French). Commentary
    on war of 1967.

HUSSEIN, King of Jordan
    Uneasy Lies the Head (London: 1962)   233 pp.
    Political autobiography.

5. Sudan

HENDERSON, K.D.D.
    The Making of the Modern Sudan: edited life and letters
    of Sir Douglas Newbold (London: Faber & Faber, 1953)
    601 pp.

    Newbold was Civil Secretary in Sudan 1939-45. Includes
    postscript on Sudan since 1945.

HILL, Richard
    A Biographical Dictionary of the Sudan (London: Frank
    Cass, 1967) Second edition.

MAHGOUB, Mohamed Ahmed
<u>Democracy on Trial: reflections on Arab and African pol-
itics</u> (London: Deutsch, 1974)

Personal account by former Sudanese prime minister;
includes two chapters on Sudan.

ARABIA, IRAN AND THE GULF

A. POLITICAL HISTORY

INGRAMS, Harold
Arabia and the Isles   (London: Murray, 1942)

Classical study of southwestern Arabia.

1. Gulf States

KOCHWASSER, Friedrich H.
Kuwait (Tubingen and Basel: Verlag, 1969)   420 pp.

Substantial survey in German of history and infrastructure of state of Kuwait.

LANDEN, Robert Geran
Oman Since 1845: disruptive modernization in a tradition-
al Arab society (Princeton, N.J.: Princeton University
Press, 1967)   488 pp.
Bibliography.

Important interpretative study by American scholar of
impact of modernizing influences on Oman from mid-1800s
to discovery of oil in 1963. Based on extensive use of
Omani chronicles and official archival sources, work is
organized around four themes: Oman and the old order in
Persian Gulf; impact of early economic and technological
modernization; consolidation of British political para-
mountcy in Oman and Persian Gulf; Oman's political accommodation to new age.

MANN, Clarence
Abu Dhabi: birth of an oil sheikhdom (Beirut: Khayats,
1969) Revised edition. 153 pp.

Informative history of Abu Dhabi from 1800s to mid-1960s.
Discusses ruling family, leading tribes, controversy over
al-Buraymi, impact of oil wealth on sheikhdom, and role
of British. Contains much useful information in appendices relating to above subjects.

2. Iran

ARMANJANI, Yahya
    Iran (Englewood Cliffs, N.J.: Prentice-Hall, 1972)

    Historical background to modern Iran with feeling for
    Iranian culture.

AVERY, P.W.
    Modern Iran (London: 1965) Second edition.

    Outstanding historical study of 20th century Iran (inclu-
    ding early chapters on 19th century) which surveys poli-
    tical development, particularly in response to Western
    impact.

BANANI, A.
    The Modernization of Iran 1921-41 (Stanford, Calif.:
    Stanford University Press, 1961)

    Useful account of work of Reza Shah.

Cambridge History of Iran, Volumes I-V (Cambridge: Cambridge
    University Press, 1968-)

    Volume I provides survey of land and people which is val-
    uable for study of modern politics. Subsequent volumes
    follow historical succession.

STEVENS, Roger
    The Land of the Great Sophy (London: Methuen, 1962)
    291 pp.

    General survey written by former British ambassador and
    intended for visitors to Iran (providing in its second
    part a high class guide book), it is one of best intro-
    ductions to history and culture of Iran.

3. Saudi Arabia, Yemen and Aden

GAVIN, R.J.
    Aden under British Rule 1839-1967 (London: Hurst, 1975)
    472 pp.

    Scholarly historical study; footnotes provide valuable
    review of source material.

LITTLE, Tom
    South Arabia: arena of conflict (London: Pall Mall Press,
    1968)   196 pp.
    Bibliography.

    Political history of South Arabia up to independence of
    People's Republic of South Yemen in 1967. Discusses

creation and failure of federation; independence struggle;
relations between different Arab groups; role of Egypt
in conflict; final result of struggle.

SCHMIDT, Dana Adams
Yemen: the unknown war   (London: Bodley Head, 1968)
316 pp.

Valuable journalist's account of Yemen War.

TREVASKIS, Sir Kennedy
Shades of Amber: a South Arabian episode (London: Hutchinson, 1968)   256 pp.

Personal account of political history of Aden from 1951-
67, written by British Agent of that period. Subjective
analysis of British presence in South Arabia, creation
of South Arabian Federation, relations with other Middle
Eastern states are all considered. Takes critical view
of eventual British withdrawal from Aden.

WENNER, Manfred W.
Modern Yemen 1918-66 (Baltimore, Md.: Johns Hopkins
University Press, 1967)   231 pp.
Bibliography (extensive, in several languages).

This book remains best scholarly work on history of
Yemen in this century. Treats in considerable detail
the position and role of Imamate, opening of country to
foreign influences, founding and first years of republic
in 1962.

B. POLITICAL SYSTEMS, GOVERNMENT

The Gulf: implications of British withdrawal (Special Report
Series No. 8; Washington, D.C.: The Center for Strategic
and International Studies, Georgetown University, 1969)
110 pp.

Compact study which grew out of conference of British and
American specialists in Washington, 1968. Concerned
primarily with assessing short and long term prospects
for stability in the Gulf as result of 1968 announcement
by British government of its intention to withdraw from
the Gulf by 1971. Book is still of interest to those
seeking understanding of present day problems bearing on
Western interests in the area; it typifies concerns of
those who perceive 'power vacuum' in the area.

HOLDEN, David
    Farewell to Arabia (New York: Walker, 1966)   243 pp.

    Written by talented British journalist; provides thought-
    ful and provocative account of people and politics in
    Arabian peninsula; based largely on first-hand observa-
    tion of events in mid-1960s and interviews with key per-
    sonalities.

HOPWOOD, D., ed.
    The Arabian Peninsula: society and politics (Totowa,
    Rowman and Littlefield, 1972)   320 pp.
    Bibliography.

    Bibliographical essay by editor is followed by fourteen
    conference papers on historical topics, on political
    developments and international relations, on society and
    culture, and on economics. Well-known contributors in-
    clude Abu Hakima, Bathurst, Burrell, Kelly, Penrose,
    Sayigh, Stoakes and Wilkinson.

LORIMER, J.G.
    Gazetteer of the Persian Gulf, Oman and Central Arabia
    Six volumes. (Calcutta: India Office, 1915; Farnborough,
    Eng.: Gregg International, 1970)

    Compiled mainly from data collected by British officials
    during early 20th century, these volumes constitute
    compendia of information that is still valuable for its
    insights into background of geography, economics, tribes,
    leading families, etc.

SANGER, Richard H.
    The Arabian Peninsula (Ithaca, N.Y.: Cornell University
    Press, 1954)   295 pp.

    General survey concerned with most of countries of
    peninsula.

YOUNG, T. Cuyler, ed.
    Middle East Focus: the Persian Gulf (Proceedings of the
    Twentieth Annual Near East Conference; Princeton, N.J.:
    Princeton University Press, 1969)   220 pp.

    Collection of papers read at symposium in October 1968.
    Volume gives sufficient attention to historical, cultur-
    al, economic and social aspects to make it a well-balanced
    and interesting introduction to the area. Contributors
    include Badeau, Kelly, Landau, Liebesny, El Mallakh,
    Rentz, Smolansky, Verrier, Young.

1. Gulf States

ANTHONY, John Duke
Arab States of the Lower Gulf: people, politics, petroleum
(Washington, D.C.: 1975)
Bibliography.

Invaluable survey of Bahrain, Qatar and United Arab Emirates.

FENELSON, Kevin
The Trucial States: a brief economic survey (Beirut:
Khayats, 1969)   Second edition.

Brief and readable survey of economies of Abu Dhabi,
Dubai, Ra's al-Khayma, Sharja, 'Ajman, Umm al-Qaywayn,
Fujayra. Based on author's intimate acquaintance with
developments in area and on government reports and data
from 1968 census conducted by Trucial States Council.

FENELSON, Kevin
The United Arab Emirates: an economic and social survey
(London: Longmans, 1973)   160 pp.

Sequel to author's volumes on Trucial States, with considerable body of illustrative material on developments
since achievement of independence in 1971.

FREETH, Zahra, and Victor WINSTONE
Kuwait: prospect and reality (New York: Crane, Russak
and Co., 1972)   229 pp.
Bibliography.

Authors are an industrial writer and daughter f former
advisor to Kuwaiti government; main value of book lies
in sections on Kuwait history before discovery of oil,
and in chapters on politics and economics and 'looking
to the future' which provide insight into role of oil
in bringing about change within Kuwaiti society and in
orientation of country's foreign and defense policies.

HAWLEY, Donald
The Trucial States (London: George Allen & Unwin, 1970;
New York: Humanities Press, 1971)   268 pp.
Bibliography.

Written by British diplomat with long experience in
Lower Gulf and Oman, book is good introduction to study
of seven sheikhdoms, formerly known as Trucial States,
which combined to form United Arab Emirates. Includes
detailed reconstruction of historical development up to
early 1970s, discussion of oil, economic development,

Bairaymi dispute, negotiations leading to establishment
of federation in 1971; appendices constitute one-third
of book with information on various cultural, economic
and social aspects of societies examined.

MERTZ, Robert Anton
Education and Manpower in the Arabian Gulf (Washington,
D.C.: American Friends of the Middle East, 1972) 226 pp.

Studies interrelationship between human and economic
development in Bahrain, Qatar, United Arab Emirates and
Oman. Based mainly on field research plus government
statistics.

MORRIS, J.
Sultan in Oman (London: Faber & Faber, 1957)   166 pp.

Impressionistic survey based on visit at time of Bairaymi
dispute.

Oman (Musqat: Department of Information, 1972)   55 pp.
Bibliography.

First book-length account of sultanate to be published
since July 1970 coup d'etat which took Oman out of its
long isolation. Highly readable and sympathetic account
portraying Oman against historical background; supplemented by more than 40 photos. Appendices provide more
information on geography, population, petroleum development, foreign trade, government structure, etc.

SADIK, Muhammad T., and William P. SNAVELY
Bahrain, Qatar and the United Arab Emirates: colonial
past, present problems and future prospects (Lexington,
Mass.: Lexington Books, 1972)   255 pp.
Bibliography.

Best single work to appear on nine Lower Gulf sheikhdoms
since they received independence in 1971; product of
extensive field research by two experts in development
problems. Includes over 100 charts and tables, with
much previously unavailable information.

SKEET, Ian
Muscat and Oman: the end of an era (London: Faber &
Faber, 1974) 224 pp.

Historical and political survey.

2. Iran

BINDER, Leonard
  Iran: political development in a changing society
  (Berkeley: University of California Press, 1962)

  Invaluable account of Iranian politics following World
  War II, emphasizing importance of market exchange as an
  underlying supposition of political exchange. Opens
  with model-building chapter which some readers find dis-
  pensable.

SMITH, Harvey H., et al.
  Area Handbook for Iran (Foreign Area Studies, American
  University; Washington, D.C.: USGPO, 1971)   653 pp.
  Bibliography.

  One of series of handbooks containing considerable detailed information. Comprises chapters on governmental
  and social structure, political attitudes and values,
  national defense and economy. Excellent data and good
  collection of maps. Series also includes handbooks for
  Iraq, peripheral states of Arabian peninsula, Saudi
  Arabia.

WILBER, Donald N.
  Contemporary Iran (London: Thames & Hudson, 1963) 224 pp.

  Following descriptive and historical introduction, book
  discusses 'turbulent present' in somewhat superficial
  manner.

WILBER, Donald N.
  Iran: past and present (Princeton, N.J.: Princeton University Press, 1958)   312 pp.

  Substantial account of politics and government at time
  of writing; illuminated by historical and cultural background.

YAR-SHATER, Ehsan, ed.
  Iran Faces the Seventies (New York: Praeger, 1971)
  380 pp.

  Collection of essays on major aspects of Persian politics
  and society including amongst others, land reform (Lambton), politics during 1960s (Hafez Farmayan), and foreign relations (Hurewitz).

3. Saudi Arabia, Yemen and Aden

INGRAMS, Harold
  The Yemen: Imams, rulers and revolutions   (London:
  Murray, 1963)   164 pp.

  General survey by former British diplomat.

MACRO, Eric
  Yemen and the Western World   (London: C. Hurst, 1968)
  150 pp.
  Bibliography.

  Historical survey provides introduction to study of
  coup of 1962 and its aftermath.

TWITCHELL, K.S.
  Saudi Arabia   (Princeton, N.J.: Princeton University
  Press, 1958)   280 pp.

  General survey directed primarily to study of development of natural resources with also provides account of
  construction and organization of Saudi state.

C. POLITICAL PARTIES, INTEREST GROUPS AND IDEOLOGIES

MILES, S.M.
  The Countries and Tribes of the Persian Gulf   (London:
  S.M. Harrison & Sons, 1919; London: Frank Cass, 1966)
  580 pp.

  Two volumes in one which first appeared more than 50
  years ago. Several sections are still of considerable
  interest today: history of commerce in Gulf and rise of
  Al Bu Sa'id dynasty of Oman. Includes detailed portraits
  of places in Oman which have changed very little in
  meantime.

1. Gulf States

EL MALLAKH, Raqaei
  Economic Development and Regional Cooperation: Kuwait
  (Chicago: University of Chicago Press, 1968)   265 pp.
  Bibliography.

  Important contribution to history of Kuwait's economic
  development and its role in promoting economic and social
  change in other Arab states; indispensable background
  reading for appraising nature and direction of country's
  future development policies.

2. Iran

AMUZEGAR, Jahangir, and Muhammad Ali FEKFRAT
Iran: Economic Development under Dualistic Conditions
(Chicago: University of Chicago Press, 1971)   177 pp.
Bibliography.

Most recent account written by two Iranian scholars of
conditions under which economic growth has occurred in
Iran over past two decades; text focuses primarily on
petroleum industry and more traditional sectors of economy and is supplemented by useful data.

ARFA, Hassan
The Kurds: an historical and political study   (London:
Oxford University Press, 1966)   178 pp.

Account devoted primarily to Kurds of Persian Azerbaijan
but touching also on Iraq and Turkey; written by late
Chief of Staff of the Iranian Army.

BILL, James Alban
The Politics of Iran: groups, classes and modernization
(Columbus, Ohio: Charles E. Merrill, 1972)   156 pp.
Bibliography.

Analysis of interaction between interest groups and
social classes and impact that both forces have on development of Iran; may be regarded, within its carefully
defined limits, as definitive work on nature and modal-
ities of political change in present-day Iran.

COTTAM, R.W.
Nationalism in Iran   (Pittsburgh: University of Pittsburgh Press, 1964)   332 pp.

Full analysis of tribes, base for nationalism, separatist
movements, and nationalism as modern movement.

LAMBTON, A.K.S.
Landlord and Peasant in Persia   (London: Oxford Univer-
sity Press, 1953)   459 pp.
Bibliography.

Authoritative account; includes glossary.

LAMBTON, A.K.S.
The Persian Land Reform   (Oxford: Clarendon Press, 1969)
385 pp.

Sequel to the above; provides account of politics of
land reform. Includes glossary.

ZABIH, S.
The Communist Movement in Iran   (Berkeley: University of
California Press, 1966)   268 pp.

Studies both communist movement in Iran and in general,
communist doctrine on social and national revolution in
the East.   Very detailed; chronologically organized.

ZONIS, Marvin
The Political Elite of Iran   (Princeton, N.J.: Princeton
University Press, 1971)   389 pp.

Detailed description and analysis of many of key actors
in Iranian political system, by University of Chicago
political scientist; covers background, recruitment,
training and attitudes of important decision-makers
within Iran government.

3. Saudi Arabia, Yemen and Aden

BUJRA, Abdalla S.
The Politics of Stratification: a study of political
change in a South Arabian town   (New York: Oxford University Press, 1971)   196 pp.
Bibliography.

Comprehensive study by Kenyan anthropologist of transformation of political attitudes and values in Hadramaut
region of People's Democratic Republic of Yemen. Based
on extensive field work carried out in 1960s, is one of
few serious scholarly works on political change at
village level of any country in Arabian peninsula.

D. BIOGRAPHIES, MEMOIRS, SPEECHES, WRITINGS
BY POLITICAL LEADERS

2. Iran

PAHLAVI, H.J.M. Mohammed Reza Shah, Shah of Iran
Mission for my Country   (London: 1960)   335 pp.

Political autobiography.

3. Saudi Arabia, Yemen and Aden

GAURY, Gerald de
Feisal, King of Saudi Arabia   (London: Arthur Barber;
New York: Praeger, 1967)   140 pp.
Bibliography.

Sympathetic portrait by former British diplomat and
soldier, based on much personal material.

E. EXTERNAL RELATIONS

ALBARHANA, Husain M.
The Legal Status of the Arabian Gulf States: a study of
their treaty relations and their international problems
(Manchester: Manchester University Press, 1968) 351 pp.
Bibliography.

Written by official of Bahrain government; includes sections detailing British treaty relations with and international status of Arab Gulf States and provides much
information of political histories of these states, their
constitutional structure and their territorial claims
and boundary problems. Appendices include texts of various treaties and agreements and five maps.

ANTHONY, John D., Ishwer OJHA, and John STEEVES
The Great Powers, the Indian Ocean and the Gulf (Wash-
ington, D.C.: The Middle East Institute, 1972) 21 pp.
Mimeo.

Three essays discussing geo-strategic aspects and in-
creasing international significance of Gulf, Indian
Ocean area and Indian sub-continent. (1)'The Lower Gulf
States: new roles in regional affairs'(Anthony); (2)'South
Asia Today: an area caught in great power rivalry'
(Steeves); (3)'The Role of China' (Ohja).

BURRELL, R.M., and Alvin COTTRELL
Iran, the Arabian Peninsula and the Indian Ocean (New
York: National Strategy Information Center, 1972) 46 pp.
Bibliography.

Brief essay by two scholars on various geo-strategic
problems. Chapters include: 'The Persian Gulf and its
Oil Revenues', 'Iranian Policy Objectives', 'The Arabian
Shore: problems of stability', and 'The US, Russia and
the Role of Naval Power in the Indian Ocean'.

BURRELL, R.M.
The Persian Gulf (Washington, D.C.: Center for Strategic
and International Studies, Georgetown University, 1972)
81 pp.

Competent survey of principal issues and disputes bearing on political stability and prospects for peaceful
change in Gulf; presents succinctly some of Gulf's more
complex international and intraregional problems with
important political and economic implications.

CHURBA, Joseph
Conflict and Tension among the States of the Persian
Gulf, Oman and South Arabia (Foreign Affairs Research
Paper No. 15346-P; Documentary Research Study AU-204-71-
IPD; Montgomery, Ala.: The Institute for Professional
Development, Air University, Maxwell Air Force Base,
1971)   74 pp.

Useful survey of major problems affecting political stability within and among peripheral states of Arabian
peninsula.

KELLY, J.B.
Eastern Arabian Frontiers (New York: Praeger, 1964)
319 pp.
Bibliography.

Detailed study of background to conflicting claims of
Saudi Arabia, Abu Dhabi and Oman to region of al-Buraymi
and other areas in eastern Arabian peninsula. Author
does not, on the whole, support validity of Saudis' various claims.

MONROE, Elizabeth
The Changing Balance of Power in the Persian Gulf (New
York: American Universities Field Staff, Inc., 1972)
69 pp.

Based on conference held in Rome in 1972 to examine
range of problems related to future of Gulf. Participants
were mainly British and American specialists on Middle
East and energy questions and anaylzes implications of
recent political and socio-economic changes in the area.

PAGE, Stephen
The USSR and Arabia: the development of Soviet policies
and attitudes towards the countries of the Arabian peninsula (London: Central Asian Research Centre, 1971)
136 pp.
Bibliography.

Seminal work on historical evolution of drives and aims
behind Soviet policy in the peninsula; by Canadian political scientist who has utilized extensive original
source material in Russian.

United States Interests in and Policy Toward the Persian Gulf
(Hearings of the Subcommittee on the Near East, Committee
on Foreign Affairs, House of Representatives; Washington,
D.C.: USGPO, 1972)   134 pp.

Includes testimony by US government officials and representatives of petroleum industry; also includes state-
ment by James E. Akins at 8th Arab Oil Congress of June
1972 and articles by El-Mallakh, Berry and Anthony.

1. Gulf States

DICKSON, H.R.P.
Kuwait and her Neighbours   (London: George Allen & Unwin,
1956)   628 pp.

Early extensive survey by former British political agent
in the Gulf.

2. Iran

RAMAZANI, Rouhollah K.
The Persian Gulf: Iran's role   (Charlottesville, Va.:
University of Virginia Press, 1972)   157 pp.
Bibliography.

Concise and well-researched account of development of
Iranian interests in and policies towards the Gulf;
appendices dealing with resolution of Iranian claim to
Bahrain and concerning problem of Abu Marsa Island and
two Tunbs Islands.

ISRAEL

A. POLITICAL HISTORY

BENTWICH, Norman
    <u>Israel</u> (London: Ernest Benn, 1952) 224 pp.

    Successor to author's work on Palestine. Provides general survey based on historical account.

HADAWI, Sami
    <u>Bitter Harvest: Palestine between 1914-67</u> (New York: New World Press, 1967) 355 pp.

    Written by Palestinian Arab, provides historical account of creation of state of Israel, Arab refugee problem, Arabs under Israeli rule, and commentary on Israel's international position.

HUREWITZ, J C.
    <u>The Struggle for Palestine</u> (New York: W.W. Norton Co., 1950) 403 pp.

    Historical account of British mandate over Palestine, Jewish and Arab policies, Zionist activity and policies of Arab states; UN involvement and international politics of creation of the state.

KOESTLER, Arthur
    <u>Promise and Fulfilment: Palestine 1917-49</u> (London: Macmillan, 1949) 335 pp.

    Narrative concluding with chapters on Hebrew language and politics and culture of new state.

MARLOWE, John
    <u>The Seat of Pilate: an account of the Palestine mandate</u> (London: Cresset Press, 1959) 289 pp.

    Very readable narrative account of events from Balfour Declaration to creation of state of Israel.

POLK, William R., et al.
  The Struggle for Palestine: backdrop to tragedy (Boston: 1957)

  Successfully brings together Arab, Jewish and American views of origins of state of Israel.

STEIN, Leonard
  The Balfour Declaration (London: Vallentine-Mitchell, 1961)   681 pp.

  Standard, detailed account of background and negotiations which led to Balfour Declaration.

STOCK, Ernest
  Israel on the Road to Sinai (Ithaca, N.Y.: Cornell University Press, 1967)   284 pp.
  Bibliography.

  Account of events leading up to Sinai campaign, 1956; with postscript on war of 1967. Account of diplomacy to some extent outdated.

B. POLITICAL SYSTEMS, GOVERNMENT

BERMANT, Chaim
  Israel (London: Thames & Hudson, 1967)   224 pp.

  General survey in the 'New Nations' series. Illustrated. Glossary and who's who.

ECKARDT, Alice and Roy
  Encounter with Israel: a challenge to conscience (New York: Association Press, 1970)   304 pp.

  Wide ranging survey, from history of Palestine to politics and society of Israel. Argues 'moral' case throughout - Jewish rights to Israel and rights of Arabs within Jewish state.

EISENSTADT, S.N., Rivkah BAR YOSEF, and Chaim ADLER, eds.
  Integration and Development in Israel (London: Pall Mall Press, 1970; New York: Praeger, 1970)   703 pp.
  Bibliography.

  Large collection of essays, some published elsewhere, relating to economics, politics and sociology of Israel.

EISENSTADT, S.N.
Israeli Society (London: Weidenfeld & Nicolson, 1967)
451 pp.

Authoritative study of economic structure, social organization and stratification, education, political structure and institutions.

PRITTIE, Terence
Israel: miracle in the desert (London: Pall Mall Press,
1967) 246 pp.

Journalist's general survey, illustrated, which argues
the success and legitimacy of Israel. Written before
six-day war.

SEGRE, V.D.
Israel: a society in transition (London: Oxford University Press, 1971) 227 pp.

Studies evolution of Jewish community from traditional
society of Yishuv to modern industrial state, arguing
that process is comparable to any other process of modernization in other states.

C. POLITICAL PARTIES, INTEREST GROUPS AND IDEOLOGIES

ARIAN, Alan
The Choosing People: voting behaviour in Israel (Case
Western Reserve University, 1973)
Bibliography.

Substantial analysis of voting behaviour, based on interviews. Valuable appendices showing interview methods.

ARIAN, Alan
Ideological Change in Israel (Cleveland, Ohio: Case
Western Reserve University Press, 1968) 220 pp.

Studies and compares ideologies of secular political
parties and of kibbutz movement.

AVNERY, Uri
Israel without Zionists: a plea for peace in the Middle
East (London: Macmillan, 1968) 215 pp.

Author is journalist and member of Knesset who urges
'great Semitic confederacy putting an end to the Zionist
chapter'. Useful insights on origin, nature and history
of state.

BENTWICH, Norman
Israel: two fateful years 1967-69   (London: Elek, 1970)
115 pp.

Surveys background, from Israeli point of view, leading
to six-day war and comments on problems arising from it.

CURTIS, Michael, and Mordechai S. CHERTOFF, eds.
Israel: social structure and change   (New Brunswick, N.J.:
Rutgers University Press, 1973)

Collection of essays originating from conferences held by
American Association for Peace in the Middle East and
American Histadruth Exchange Institute.

LANDAU, Jacob
The Arabs in Israel: a political study   (London: Oxford
University Press, 1969)   300 pp.

Scholarly study of political organization, elections,
participation in parties and trade unions and political
leadership.

LAQUEUR, Walter
A History of Zionism   (London: Weidenfeld & Nicolson,
1972)   640 pp.

Standard history of Zionist movement.

PERLMUTTER, A.
Military and Politics in Israel: nation-building and role
expansion   (London: Frank Cass, 1969)   161 pp.

Sociological study of Israeli army; an account of civil-
military relations and role of army in determining foreign and defense policies.

SCWARZ, Walter
The Arabs in Israel   (London: Faber & Faber, 1959) 172 pp.

Impressionistic, informative account of subject.

SHOKEID, Moshe
The Dual Heritage: immigrants from the Atlas Mountains
in an Israeli village   (Manchester: Manchester University
Press, 1971)   245 pp.
Bibliography.

Studies political and family relationships.

TALMON, Jacob
   Israel among the Nations   (London: Weidenfeld & Nicolson,
   1970)   199 pp.

   Three essays: Jews between revolution and counter-revolution describes part taken by Jews in 19th and 20th century European political movements; types of Jewish self-
   awareness is retrospective view of Herzl's Jewish State
   and its impact; Israel among the nations is commentary
   on six-day war of 1967.

ZWEIG, Ferdinand
   Israel: the sword and the harp   (London: Heinemann, 1969)
   326 pp.

   Sociological observations grouped around 'controversial
   themes in Israeli society' including 'mystique of violence and mystique of redemption'. Studies identity and
   self-image, status and stratification, two mystiques,
   encounters and dialogues with Arabs and with major powers.

ZWEIG, Ferdinand
   The Israeli Worker (New York: Herzl and Sharon Press,
   1959)

   Sociological study of Israeli working class, trade union
   and political organization.

D. BIOGRAPHIES, MEMOIRS, SPEECHES, WRITINGS
BY POLITICAL LEADERS

BEN-GURION, David
   Israel: years of challenge   (London: Anthony Blond,
   1963)   240 pp.

   Personal account of establishment of Israeli state, bor-
   der tensions leading to Sinai war of 1956 and subsequent
   Israeli withdrawal.

BEN-GURION, David
   My Talks with Arab Leaders   (Jerusalem: Keder Books,
   1972)   343 pp.

   Covers period from before World War I to 1962.

BEN-GURION, David
   Rebirth and Destiny of Israel   (London: Yoseloff, 1959)
   538 pp.

   Edited and translated from Hebrew by M. Nurock. Historical account valuable for exposition of author's political views.

BEN-GURION, David
Recollections   (London: Macdonald Unit Seventy-five,
1970)   215 pp.

Edited by Thomas Bransten.   Series of reminiscences from
early years to after war of 1967.

BERLIN, Sir Isaiah
Chaim Weizmann   (New York: Farrar, Strauss and Cudahy,
1958)   60 pp.

Constructed from Herbert Samuel Lecture in Jerusalem
and Weizmann Memorial Lecture at Leeds.

DAYAN, Moshe
Diary of the Sinai Campaign   (London: Weidenfeld & Nicolson, 1965)   235 pp.

Account of 1956 campaign by one of its commanders; valuable for its comments on origins of the war.

EBAN, Abba
Israel in the World   (New York: Thomas Yoseloff, 1966)
70 pp.

Two television interviews in March 1965.

EBAN, Abba
My Country: the story of modern Israel   (London: Weidenfeld & Nicolson, 1972)   304 pp.

Illustrated account of first twenty-five years of Israel.

EBAN, Abba
Voice of Israel   (New York: Horizon Press, 1957)   304 pp.

Speeches, some from 1948 onwards, but great part from
years 1955-56.

EDELMAN, M.
Ben-Gurion   (London: Hodder & Stoughton, 1964)   214 pp.

Political biography by an admirer.

FURLONGE, Geoffrey
Palestine is My Country: the story of Musa Alami
(London: Murray, 1969)   242 pp.

Biography of founder and director of Arab Development
Society to end of 1967 war.

HOROWITZ, David
    State in the Making (New York: Knopf, 1953)   349 pp.

Translated from Hebrew by Julian Meltzer. Detailed account of negotiations leading to establishment of state of Israel by participant (who later became governor of Bank of Israel).

MANN, Peggy
    Golda: the life of Israel's Prime Minister (London: Vallentine Mitchell, 1972)   287 pp.

Personal rather than political biography.

PRITTIE, Terence
    Eshkol of Israel: the man and the nation (London: Museum Press, n.d.)   368 pp.

Informative personal and political biography.

ST. JOHN, Robert
    Eban (New York: W.H. Allen, 1973)   542 pp.

Substantial biography based on Abba Eban's archives and files and on extensive interviews.

WEIZMANN, Chaim
    Letters and Papers (London: Oxford University Press, 1968) Seven volumes.

Edited by Leonard Stein in collaboration with Gedalia Yogev. Series A, Letters: from summer 1885 to Nov. 1917.

WEIZMANN, Chaim
    Trial and Error (London: Oxford University Press, 1949)

Autobiography.

WEIZMANN, Vera
    The Impossible Takes Longer (London: Hamish Hamilton, 1967)   308 pp.

Memoirs of wife of Chaim Weizmann (as told to David Tutaev).

E. EXTERNAL RELATIONS

BRECHER, Michael
> Decisions in Israel's Foreign Policy   (London: Oxford
> University Press, 1974)   639 pp.
>
> Case studies which form a sequel to The Foreign Policy
> System of Israel (see below).

BRECHER, Michael
> The Foreign Policy System of Israel: setting, images,
> process   (London: Oxford University Press, 1972)   693 pp.
> Bibliography.
>
> Specialist study which is invaluable for light it throws
> on parties, politics and leaders.